LATIN METRE

Also available or forthcoming:

The Greek Dialects, C.D. Buck
Greek Grammar, W. Goodwin
The Greek Language, L. Palmer
Greek Metre, D.S. Raven
The Greek Particles, J. Denniston
Greek Prose Style, J. Denniston
Syntax of the Moods & Tenses of the Greek Verb, W. Goodwin
Latin Grammar, Gildersleeve & Lodge
The Latin Language, L. Palmer
A New Latin Syntax, E. Woodcock

LATIN METRE

BY

D.S. Raven

Published by Bristol Classical Press
General Editor: John H. Betts

First published in 1965 by Faber & Faber Ltd

Paperback edition published in 1998 by
Bristol Classical Press
an imprint of
Gerald Duckworth & Co. Ltd
61 Frith Street
London W1D 3JL
e-mail: inquiries@duckworth-publishers.co.uk
Website: www.ducknet.co.uk

Reprinted 1999, 2001

A catalogue record for this book is available
from the British Library

ISBN 1-85399-564-9

Contents

PREFACE   *page*   11

INTRODUCTORY NOTE   13

ABBREVIATIONS   15

1   LATIN VERSE STRUCTURE, AND ITS HISTORY   17
     § 1   Influence of Greek models on the Roman poets
     2–5   Greek prototypes
     6–9   Simplicity of Roman practice and adaptation; questions
           of performance

2   QUANTITY, PROSODY AND THE BASIC
    RHYTHMS   22
     § 10–11   Quantity and accent
     12–15   Principles of quantity: quantity and tempo, 12;
               rules of quantity, 13; 'brevis brevians' law, 14;
               elision and hiatus, 15
     16–19   Basic feet; the metron, caesura and diaeresis;
               'doubtful position'

3   WORD-ACCENT; SATURNIAN VERSE; THE
    INFLUENCE OF ACCENT THROUGHOUT LATIN
    VERSE LITERATURE   31
     § 20–21   Significance and principles of word-accent
     22–28   Accent in the history of Latin literature: saturnian
               verse, 22; accent in the 'classical' period, 26; accent in
               mediaeval Latin verse, 28

Contents

4 IAMBIC AND TROCHAIC VERSE   41

§ 29 Division into 'types' of iambic and trochaic verse

Left-hand pages   *Right-hand pages*

Type A: strict lyric usage   *Type B: early Roman drama,*
after the Greek pattern   *etc.*

§ 30A Iambic and trochaic   § 30B–31B Iambic and
metron: 'type A'   trochaic metron: 'type
                                      B'; nomenclature; restric-
                                      tions of accent

32A–39A Iambic tri-   32B–39B Iambic senarius:
meter: 'pure' iambic   general rules, 32B;
trimeter, 33A; 'normal'   principles of word-
trimeter, 34A; silver   division, 36B–38B;
Latin trimeter, 35A;   scheme, 39B
principles of word-
division, 36A–38A;
scheme, 39A

40A–45A Other iambic   40B–46B Other iambic
lengths: iambic dimeter,   lengths: iambic quater-
40A; scazon, 42A; cata-   narius, 40B; iambic
lexis in iambics, 44A;   octonarius, 43B; iambic
departures from the   septenarius, 44B; de-
metron-scheme, 45A   partures from the metron-
                                      scheme, 45B; reizianum
                                      and versus reizianus, 46B

47A–50A Trochaic tetra-   47B–50B Trochaic sept-
meter catalectic: general   enarius: general rules,
rules, 47A; principles of   47B; principles of word-
word-division, 48A–49A;   division, 48B–49B;
scheme, 50A   scheme, 50B

51A–55A Other trochaic   52B–55B Other trochaic
lengths: trochaic scazon,   lengths: trochaic quater-
51A; trochaic dimeter,   narius, 52B; trochaic
52A; trochaic dimeter   octonarius, 53B; trochaic
catalectic, 54A; ithy-   quaternarius catalectic,
phallic, 55A   54B; ithyphallic, etc., 55B

56A Iambic and trochaic   56B Iambic and trochaic
lengths among other   lengths among other
metres   metres

Contents

5   DACTYLIC VERSE AND SIMPLE DACTYLIC
   COMPOUNDS   90

   § 57–59   Basic rhythm and metron; catalexis

   § 60–77   *Dactylic Hexameter*:   90
   60–61   Basic scheme and occasional variants
   62–64   Development and rules for word-division: word-
       accent, 63; classes of hexameter writing, 64
   65–69   Centre of line: main central caesura, 66; secondary
       principles, 67–68; word-accent, 69
   70–76   End of line: (1) early usage—Ennius, 70; Lucretius,
       71; (2) developed type—general principles, 72–73;
       Greek imitations, 74; word-accent, 75; (3) conversa-
       tional type, 76
   77   General flow of hexameter verse

   § 78–89   *Elegiac Couplet*:   103
   78–80   Description of pentameter and of elegiac couplet
   81   Structure of hexameter in elegiac verse
   82–83   Structure of pentameter—general: central caesura, 83
   84–88   Structure of pentameter—line-ending: (1) in
       Catullus, 84; (2) in Propertius and Tibullus, 85;
       (3) in Ovid, 86; (4) in later poets, 87; word-accent,
       88
   89   General flow of elegiac verse

   § 90–96   *Dactyls in Lyric Verse*:   110
   90–91   Typical lengths; all-dactylic stanza forms, 91
   92–96   Dactyls mingled with other metres: simple alterna-
       tions, 92; closer intermingling, and archilochean
       stanzas, 93–96

6   ANAPAESTIC VERSE   115

   § 97–98   The rhythm and metron
   99–102   Anapaestic systems—'strict' type: in Seneca, 100–
       101; catalexis—the paroemiac, 102
   103–104   Anapaestic systems in Plautus
   105–108   Longer anapaestic lines in Plautus: octonarius,
       106; septenarius, 107

7   BACCHIAC AND CRETIC VERSE   123

   § 109   The basic rhythms
   110–114   Bacchiac verse: the metron and its variations,
       110–112; catalexis and other curtailment, 113;
       diaeresis, 114

Contents

115–120 Cretic verse: the metron and its variations, 115–117; catalexis and other curtailment, 118; diaeresis, 119; cretics in prose rhythm, 120

121 Bacchiac and cretic verse in comic lyric

8 IONIC VERSE   129

§ **122–123** Basic ionic metron, and its simple use; anacreontic, 123

124–125 Special lengths: galliambic, 124; sotadean, 125

126 Ionics mingled with other metres

9 AEOLIC VERSE   133

§ **127** Application of the term 'aeolic'

128–129 Elements of aeolic verse: the nucleus — ˇˇ — and its expansions, 128; syllables preceding and following the nucleus, 129

130–133 Construction of aeolic lengths: lines built on the nucleus — ˇˇ — and its expansions, 131–132 (tabulated); contraction in the nucleus, 133

134–141 Individual aeolic lengths and stanzas: reizianum, 135; phalaecian hendecasyllable, 136; glyconic stanzas, 137; asclepiad stanzas, 138; sapphic stanza, 139; 'greater sapphic', 140; alcaic stanza, 141

142–145 Aeolic in dramatic lyric: in comedy, 142; in Seneca, 143–145

INDEX A *Names of Various Metrical Forms and Terms*   151

INDEX B *References to Authors and Passages*   164

APPENDIX A *A Note on Prose Rhythm and Ciceronian 'Clausulae'*   169

APPENDIX B *Metrical Notes on Selected Authors*   173
Introductory note: (1) Early Roman poets—selections from Ernout's *Recueil*; (2) Plautus; (3) Terence; (4) Catullus; (5) *Appendix Vergiliana*; (6) Horace; (7) Phaedrus; (8) Persius; (9) Seneca; (10) Petronius; (11) Statius; (12) Martial; (13) Ausonius

Preface

The quantitative metres of the ancient Greek and Latin languages are basically by no means hard to understand; but students have long been accustomed to recoil from any study of them with a quite unjustifiable alarm. This alarm is partly caused, perhaps, by the formidable array of technical terms mustered by the ancient metricians and reproduced in modern grammars and editions. Yet such terms are often of no use towards an understanding of this subject, and it should be possible for undergraduates—and indeed for classical students in the schools—to ignore many of these technicalities, and yet reach a reasonable understanding of the rhythmical flow of classical Greek and Latin verse.

My previous *Greek Metre* was produced with this aim in mind, and the present work is now offered as a companion volume at the same level. Following my practice in the former work, I have enclosed advanced and non-essential information in square brackets. Technical terms are used as little as possible (although I have included an index of them for reference purposes); where they are unavoidable, they are explained as briefly as possible, and cross-referencing is used whenever it may be of service. I have also avoided the use of abbreviated notations of the type found in many works of modern scholarship[1]: these notations are concise and helpful to the slightly more advanced student, but at the elementary level which I am considering there is probably no good substitute for the most conventional and obvious signs.

The subject of Latin metre is simpler than its Greek counterpart, for reasons that are given in Ch. 1. Nevertheless it is helpful to approach the subject with *some* knowledge of Greek prototypes, and simple examples from Greek usage are quoted

[1] e.g. the metrical works of P. Maas and B. Snell.

when necessary. In general I have drawn my examples as far as possible from works widely read by students, who I hope will thus be enabled to read and scan Latin verse with some appreciation of its basically simple principles.

Many controversial subjects have perforce been dismissed in brief and categorical summaries; this is particularly regrettable in the case of the primitive verse form known as 'saturnian', where I must acknowledge with grateful thanks much wise advice from Mr. J. G. Griffith. I am also particularly indebted to Professor O. Skutsch for his kindness in reading the whole work at a later stage, in ridding it of many imperfections and suggesting a number of alterations, especially in the field of Republican drama. Previous works on Latin metre[1] have naturally moulded and affected my views and approach; but I have not consciously reproduced any material from the works of others. I hope that this introduction at least has the merit of comparative simplicity, and will show that the subject is more approachable, and indeed enjoyable, than is commonly realised.

---

[1] An excellent bibliography may be found at the end of F. Crusius' *Römische Metrik* (7th ed., revised H. Rubenbauer, München 1963); cf. also R. J. Getty in *Lustrum*, 1963, on recent contributions to the subject. Many advanced and controversial topics (such as ictus and *brevis brevians*) are best studied in German works, e.g. E. Fraenkel's *Iktus und Akzent im lateinischen Sprechvers* and O. Skutsch's *Prosodische und metrische Gesetze der Iambenkürzung*; and there is a sad lack of comprehensive English works on the subject in general, although help can sometimes be found in editions of individual authors (e.g. Bailey's of Lucretius and Wickham's of Horace). Many good examples of the prosody and metre of Roman comedy can be gathered by those with the energy to peruse W. M. Lindsay's *Early Latin Verse*; and dactylic poetry is well catered for by M. Platnauer's *Latin Elegiac Verse* and S. E. Wimbolt's *Latin Hexameter Verse*, a work intended primarily for composers but by no means confined to their needs.

Introductory Note

This book is not necessarily designed for continuous study. It may be found useful to read the first three chapters, which contain a certain amount of basic information (much of which will probably be familiar already). But the remainder of the book can be referred to as need arises in the reading of Latin verse; no individual chapter presupposes a knowledge of previous chapters (apart from the rules of quantity contained in Ch. 2)—although there is cross-referencing between chapters and sections where relevant.

The following signs are used from time to time throughout this work (besides the conventional ⏑ and — to denote short and long syllables, and ′ to indicate a syllable with word accent):

| emphasises the end of a metron (**17**), or of a metrical segment of any kind: thus used in the iambic dimeter

⏑ — ⏑ — | ⏑ — ⏑ —

it denotes the division of the line into two metra.

⋮ emphasises a point of word-division especially drawn to the reader's attention—e.g. the main 'caesura' (**18**) of the dactylic hexameter

— ⏑ ⏑ — ⏑ ⏑ — ⋮ ⏑ ⏑ — ⏑ ⏑ — ⏑ ⏑ — —

⦚ denotes hiatus (**15**)—i.e. a final syllable susceptible of elision (**15**) which is *not* actually elided: e.g.

castaneae ⦚ hirsutae

In paragraphs specifically dealing with elision (e.g. **15**), elided syllables are marked with parentheses—e.g.

monstr(um) horrend(um) inform(e) ingens

but this practice is not followed throughout the book, and in general it must be assumed that any syllable susceptible of elision is in fact elided *unless* the hiatus mark ⦚ is present.

Except for the hiatus mark, the above signs are not used in every case where they would be apposite, but only for special emphasis.

Square brackets [ ] enclose passages which may well be ignored by less advanced readers.

Abbreviations

Aesch. = Aeschylus
Aristoph. = Aristophanes
Aus. = Ausonius
Boeth. = Boethius
  Cons. = Consolatio
Cat. = Catullus
Enn. = Ennius
  Ann. = Annales
Hom. = Homer
H. = Horace
  Epod. = Epodes
  Od. = Odes
  Sat. = Satires
Juv. = Juvenal
Lucr. = Lucretius
Mart. = Martial
Ov. = Ovid
Petr. = Petronius
Pl. = Plautus
  Amph. = Amphitryo
  Asin. = Asinaria
  Aul. = Aulularia
  Bacch. = Bacchides
  Capt. = Captivi
  Cas. = Casina
  Cist. = Cistellaria
  Curc. = Curculio
  Epid. = Epidicus
  Men. = Menaechmi
  Merc. = Mercator
  Mil. = Miles Gloriosus

Most. = Mostellaria
Poen. = Poenulus
Pseud. = Pseudolus
Rud. = Rudens
Stich. = Stichus
Trin. = Trinummus
Truc. = Truculentus
Prop. = Propertius
Sen. = Seneca
  Ag. = Agamemnon
  H.F. = Hercules Furens
  H.O. = Hercules Oetaeus
  Med. = Medea
  Oct. = Octavia
  Oed. = Oedipus
  Phaedr. = Phaedra
  Phoen. = Phoenissae
  Thy. = Thyestes
  Tro. = Troades
Stat. = Statius
  Silv. = Silvae
Ter. = Terence
  Ad. = Adelphi
  Andr. = Andria
  H.T. = Heauton Timorumenos
  Hec. = Hecyra
V. = Virgil
  Aen. = Aeneid
  Catal. = Catalepton
  Ecl. = Eclogues
  Georg. = Georgics
  Priap. = Priapea
fr. = fragment

CHAPTER 1

Latin Verse Structure, and its History

The influence of Greek models on the Roman poets

1. To a very large extent, the structure of classical Latin verse is derived from that of Greek verse, whose influence is already apparent in Latin literature of the late 3rd century B.C. (Literature earlier than that of Plautus and Ennius is scanty and its evidence inconclusive; but it is at least arguable that the primitive verse-form known as saturnian—cf. 22ff.—was in origin independent of Greek influence.)

From this time onwards, the ancient Greek quantitative metres were progressively integrated into Latin verse practice. The process was not always an easy one: the Latin language presented certain fundamental differences, notably a strong word-accent (cf. Ch. 3) and an embarrassingly high proportion of quantitatively 'long' syllables (20, 26), which made certain adaptations difficult. Nevertheless, the *dialogue* metres of the Greek drama were successfully reproduced in Roman comedy, although with certain notable differences; but many of these differences were eliminated by the strict 'hellenising' influence represented, for example, by Catullus and Horace in the 1st century B.C. These poets were also successful in integrating the more complex *lyric* metres of the Greeks, and indeed Horace and his successors imposed their own, additional, rules upon them.

The dactylic hexameter of Greek epic poetry again presented difficulties, and its early appearances in Latin literature (e.g. that of Ennius) are occasionally uncouth; but this metre, too, had been integrated—again with certain new restrictions—by about the time of Catullus. The 'pentameter' (with which the hexameter combines to form the elegiac couplet) developed

17

more slowly, and did not reach a form fully satisfactory to the Romans until the Augustan age. After this age, throughout the 'silver' period of Latin poetry, there was little development in the actual metrical practice of the Roman poets.

Although the strength of the Greek influence varied to some extent from poet to poet[1], it is certainly impossible to approach the structure of Latin verse without some knowledge of its Greek ancestor. It is therefore desirable, as a preliminary, to consider briefly the broad architecture of Greek verse.

Greek prototypes

2. Very broadly speaking, Greek verse can be divided into two main types:

(a) the *stichic* type, in which lines (στίχοι), or very short groups of lines, continually repeat themselves.

(b) the genuine lyric type, whose units are much larger and less regular.

3. 'Stichic' verse is most obviously represented by the dactylic hexameter of epic poetry—a unit repeated *ad lib.* after the form *aaaaa* .... A development of this principle is seen in elegiacs, where the unit is 'distichic'—of two lines repeated *ababab* ....

Simple lyric stanzas—such as those of the Greek poets Alcaeus and Sappho—show a further development, often into four-line units which repeat themselves—e.g. *aabc, aabc* .... But the bulk of Greek lyric verse (e.g. the chorus of Greek tragedy or the odes of Pindar) is of a much more complicated structure—stanzas being built on a larger and less regular scale, and of less calculable units.

4. In the Greek drama, such complex stanzas are usually written in 'strophic' form: a pair of these stanzas match each other metrically (being known as 'strophe' and 'antistrophe'),

[1 Catullus himself was the leading figure of a clique of 'neoteric' poets whose devotion, even in detail, to Greek and 'Alexandrian' models contrasted with other poets of their age.]

and a choral ode may consist of two (or more) such matching stanzas, after the form *AABBCC* . . . . The structure of most of Pindar's odes is 'triadic': a matching strophe and antistrophe are followed by a (metrically different) 'epode', and the whole pattern is then repeated several times, *AABAAB* . . . .

5. Within the stanza, the next largest unit is the 'period'—a unit which is best ignored by beginners, since it is often extremely difficult to define with certainty. Much more obvious as a unit is the single line or 'colon', the smallest meaningful unit; although exact division into lines ('colometry') is not always certain, usually a stanza can be broken down into intelligible and familiar lengths.

Simplicity of Roman practice and adaptation

6. Such in outline is the broad architecture of Greek verse. It is remarkable (but in fact typical of the Roman approach) that the more complex structures are rarely used by the Latin poets. 'Stichic' verse (2) predominates—as in the dialogue of drama, and the dactylic hexameter and elegiac couplet; even when Greek lyric forms are adapted, they tend to be used individually in long 'stichic' series. [Even in Seneca's tragedies—which in general are closely modelled on Greek practice—the lyric portions are chiefly composed of such unvaried series—cf. **143**.]

Stanza form at a simple level is seen in the quatrains of Horace, modelled largely on the stanzas of Alcaeus and Sappho, or on similar patterns. But longer and more complex stanzas of the Greek lyric type are only rarely found—in a few passages of Seneca's tragedies, and (more notably) in the *cantica* of early Roman comedy. And even here there is little trace of the 'strophic' arrangement that is so regular in Greek lyric verse (cf. **4**)[1].

7. Even in the actual metres they employed, the Roman poets seldom approached the complexity of the Greeks. Latin metres

[1 Plautus' *cantica* have been thought to be 'strophic' to some extent; but they do not approach the close correspondence of Greek strophic verse, as may indeed be seen from the fact that their very strophic nature is disputed.]

sometimes appear complicated to the beginner (although in fact they are much simpler than is often believed); but they are far less complicated than their Greek originals, at any rate in strictly lyric verse. For example, the class of verse known as 'aeolic' (cf. Ch. 9) is confined, in Latin verse, to more straightforward forms and arrangements than those which are typical of Greek aeolic stanzas. [Furthermore, some of the more complex Greek metres do not appear at all in Latin verse—notably the compound form of verse known as dactylo-epitrite, dochmiac verse, and the practice of 'syncopation' in iambics and trochaics. (For these types, cf. my *Greek Metre*, 71ff., 91ff. and 44ff. respectively.)]

8. Latin poetry is thus simpler than Greek in the actual types of verse which it employs, and in their structural arrangements. This comparative simplicity is partly counterbalanced by severer sets of 'rules' governing various individual metres (e.g. Horace's aeolic adaptations) and much stricter principles of word-division within certain lines, as will be seen when these lines are described in detail. Such severity can be explained partly by the importance of word-accent in classical Latin, and partly by a natural tendency of the tidy Roman mind to formalise informal elements. The result of this tendency may perhaps be that Latin verse is less interesting, metrically, than Greek; but at least it becomes an easier and more approachable study for the beginner.

Questions of performance

9. Ancient metricians are not helpful towards a knowledge of performance and technique; their value lies rather in the considerable fragments of literature which they preserve in quotation form[1]. Regrettably little is known about such matters as musical accompaniment, 'tempo' and the perceptible difference

[1 Hephaestion (2nd century A.D.) is the most important of the ancient Greek metricians; for Latin metre, the most amusing *ancient* 'authority' is perhaps Terentianus Maurus, whose work (of much the same date) is written in verse.]

between rhythms. But the very simplicity of Latin lyric structures (compared with Greek, cf. **6**) implies that in such matters the Romans, for one reason and another, did not approach the advanced technique of the Greeks. (*One* reason may well lie in the fact that much Latin lyric was written for private reading or artificial recitation rather than 'live' performance.)

Abstract theorising on these issues does not lie within the scope of this book; and I have tried to confine myself to matters where the guidance of the ancient texts themselves gives us ground for reasonably sure conclusions.

CHAPTER 2

Quantity, Prosody and the Basic Rhythms

Quantity and accent

10. In English verse—and in that of other modern languages, including Italian and *mediaeval* Latin—rhythm is measured by accent. Broadly speaking, an accented syllable is regarded as 'long', and an unaccented syllable as 'short'. The sign – denotes a long syllable, ᵕ a short syllable, and one long is roughly the equivalent of two shorts, – = ᵕᵕ. This principle is very easily illustrated by the opening line of Gray's *Elegy*

The cúrfew tólls the knéll of párting dáy

where it is plain that each accented syllable is a long syllable.

11. In ancient Greek verse, and in the classical Latin verse which is largely derived from it, there is again a division into long and short syllables, but the principle of this division is entirely different, being based on the intrinsic *quantity* of different vowel-and-consonant combinations. Word accent is of secondary importance, and seems, at least in Greek, to have played little significant part in the structure of verse; at least, while there is a close correspondence in quantity between strophe and antistrophe (cf. **4**), there is no similar correspondence in word-accent.

It is, however, strikingly clear that word-accent *does* have a far greater importance, and significance, in Latin than in Greek verse. This fact, and its implications, will be considered in Ch. 3 *after* the actual principles of quantity have been examined.

Principles of quantity

12. *Quantity and 'tempo'*. Regularity of 'tempo' seems to have meant relatively little to the ancient Greeks and Romans. If we accept the equation '— = ◡◡' it is very tempting to think of the dactyl —◡◡ as a foot in 'four-time', and the iambus ◡— one in 'three-time' (though the latter presents difficulties even here, since under certain conditions a long syllable is freely substituted for the short, ⏓ —). But there are many common lines which cannot be so categorised—notably, 'aeolic' forms such as the glyconic ⏓ ⏓ — ◡◡ — ◡ —. It must therefore be concluded that the Greeks and Romans attached little importance to 'tempo', at least as we understand it in modern music.[1]

[This conclusion is at least safer than the alternative theory popular among nineteenth-century metricians. These metricians insisted that ancient verse *must* scan as regularly as their contemporary hymn-tunes, and by ruthless abandonment of the equation '— = ◡◡', by 'hurrying' short syllables and by curtailing or protracting long syllables, they contrived to fit the most complex ancient metres into schemes of 'triple' or 'quadruple' tempo. Such views are now seldom held, if for no other reason than because they are purely arbitrary and rest on practically no authority.]

13. *Rules of quantity.* The following are the main rules for determining the long or short quantity of individual syllables.

(a) All diphthongs (*ae, au,* and *ei, eu, oe* when scanned as monosyllables) are long *by nature*, e.g. *tenebrae, laudo, Proteus.*
[These diphthongs can only be shortened by the rare process of 'correption'—i.e. if left in *hiatus* (**15**) at the end of a word, before a vowel beginning the next word, e.g. (V. *Aen.* iii.211) *insulae* ⎰ *Ionio in magno*—a survival of Greek epic technique.]

(b) The single vowels *a, e, i, o, u,* (*y*), are sometimes naturally long, sometimes short: some rules for their 'natural' quantity can be found in the Latin grammars. (Final *ō* is commonly shortened in many 'silver age' poets, e.g. Juvenal, except in

[[1] The thorny question of *ictus* (a term roughly corresponding to the 'down-beat' of modern music) has, for better or for worse, been disregarded throughout this work. See footnote to Preface (p. 12), and cf. under *arsis* in Index A.]

dative and ablative cases.) Any vowel, however, is short when directly followed by another vowel and not forming a diphthong—e.g. *dĕus, audĭat* [except in some Greek derivatives (e.g. *Iŏnĭus*), certain genitive singulars in *-ĭus*, most parts of the verb *fĭo* (excluding *fĭeri, fĭerem* etc.), and 'archaic' genitives in *-āĭ* and *-ēĭ* (e.g. *materĭāĭ*)].

[Occasionally a short vowel coalesces with a following vowel (especially *i*) by the process known as *synizesis*—thus *dĕinde* and *dĕhĭnc* become *dêinde, dêhinc*; and in early Latin verse parts of *meus, tuus, suus, deus, is* often scan monosyllabically, though synizesis at the end of longer words is practically excluded from scenic poetry.]

(c) But any syllable containing a short vowel becomes long *by position* when that vowel is immediately followed by a double consonant (*x, z*) or by two or more consonants together—except in the cases listed under (d)—e.g. *dūx, ēst, ūt fīt*.

For these purposes *h* is discounted—e.g. *ĭn hostes*—but 'semi-consonantal' *i* and *u* have the full force of consonants, as in *ferūs iudex* and occasional scansions such as *gēnuă*[1]; but *qu* counts as only a single consonant—e.g. *armăque*.

It should be noted that, in early Latin verse, final *s* following a short vowel often disappears—e.g. *omnibu' rebus, fontibu' magnis.*[2]

[By the above rule, a short final vowel should strictly make a long syllable before two consonants beginning the next word; this lengthening is sometimes found in the 'rise' of the foot, e.g. Cat. 64.186   nulla fugae ratio, nullā spes and particularly in studied imitations of Greek lines (where the practice is common) e.g. V. *Aen.* viii.425   Brontesquē Steropesque

[1 This scansion exhibits another form of *synizesis*—see b. above; the converse process (*vocalic diaeresis*) may be seen in occasional scansions such as *sĭlŭāe* for the more usual *sĭlvāe*.]

[2 Certain common disyllables ending in -*ĕ* (*ille, iste, inde, unde, nempe, quippe*) sometimes scan as monosyllables in early verse—probably by a process (*apocope*) which allows them to drop their final syllable (e.g. *nemp'*) as though they were suffering normal elision (15).]

But (especially in and after the Augustan period) otherwise this lengthening is avoided, and short final vowels are hardly found in this position at all: for it seems to have been equally repugnant to the Roman poets to allow them to remain short in such a position—where again there are few examples, most of which involve words otherwise inadmissible, e.g. *nemorosă Zacynthos* (V. *Aen.* iii.270—another 'Grecism': a notable exception is *Aen.* xi.209 *ponitĕ. spes* . . .). This last restriction does not, of course, apply to the 'mute-and-liquid' combinations of (d) below.]

(d) In certain conditions listed below a short-vowelled syllable can *remain* short by position—and in early Latin verse (e.g. comedy) *always* remains short—before two consonants in the following combinations (a 'mute' and a 'liquid'):

bl, br; cl, chl, cr, chr; dr; fl, fr; gl, gr; pl, pr; tr, thr.

(In Greek derivatives there are a few cases where the second consonant may be *m* or *n*.)
either (i) when, after a final vowel, these consonants begin the next word, where indeed the doubtful syllable is nearly always short, e.g. *urbĕ fruuntur, plumbeă glans.*
[Lengthening in this position is very rare,
e.g. Cat. 4.18   et inde tot per impotentiā freta,
and may usually be seen as a conscious 'Grecism',
e.g. V. *Georg.* i.153   lappaequē tribolique
cf. on (c) above.]
or (ii) when the two consonants are in the same word as the vowel, e.g. *tenĕbrae, pătres, lăcrimae, rēplent.* Here there is a distinct *tendency* for the doubtful syllable to be short, especially in the case of *tr.*
But such shortening is *not* found
(iii) where the two consonants belong to different parts of a compound, in which case the syllable must be long: e.g. *ābrumpo.*
nor (iv) when the two consonants belong to different words—where again the syllable must be long: e.g. *āt rabidae.*

14. *'Brevis brevians' law.* The importance of accent in Latin verse (cf. Ch. 3), and the tendency of colloquial writers to fight against the preponderance of long syllables in the Latin language, are particularly evident in the law of *brevis brevians* (known also as the law of iambic shortening). This law causes certain long syllables to be shortened in comedy and other early Latin verse, and its impact can occasionally be seen in later poetry.

Literally the term *brevis brevians* implies *a short syllable shortening a succeeding long*; and the effect of the law is that a long syllable is shortened if it is *both* (a) directly preceded by a short syllable *and* (b) directly preceded and/or followed by a syllable with word-accent (**21**).

i.e. (1) ◡ — becomes ◡◡ :

thus vídēn tu	*becomes* vídĕn tu
bŏnām sententiam	*becomes* bŏnăm sententiam
quíd hōc clamoris	*becomes* quíd hŏc clamoris
and (with intervening elision)	
bĕ́n(e) ēt pudice	*becomes* bĕ́n(e) ĕt pudice

(2) ◡ — ◡́ becomes ◡◡ ◡́ :

thus vŏlūptátis	*becomes* vŏlŭptátis[1]
omnĭūm mé	*becomes* omnĭŭm mé[2].

[Some doubt still exists about the precise limits of this rule. But it may be noted that the first short syllable (the *brevians*) normally belongs to the same word as its shortened successor (the *brevianda*)—as in *vidĕn* tu, *vŏlŭp*tatis, per*didĭ* spem. Alternatively the *brevians* may be a separate monosyllabic word—as in *ut ŏccepit* or (with elision) *tib(i) ŏccepit*; but it may *not* be a final syllable of a longer word (thus ci*vis ŏccepit* is excluded), although it *may* be a *penultimate* syllable followed by elision, e.g. ci*vi(um) ŏccepit*[2].]

[[1] But vŏlúptas always, owing to the different position of the accent: *except* in the common phrase vŏlŭptás mea, where the accent seems to change again as indicated.]

[[2] The comparative rarity of this type is due to the fact that the word-division involved is practically excluded from *iambic and trochaic* verse by the 'law of the split anapaest' (**30B**). This type also poses certain advanced problems of *ictus* which are outside the scope of this work—cf. **12ⁿ**.]

Shortening by this law is particularly common in Plautus, e.g.

eg(o) ĭstuc furtum sciŏ cui factumst   (*Rud.* 956)

and the law may be held responsible for certain shortenings of final vowels which later became standard usage e.g. *egŏ, modŏ.* [It must be remembered, however, that silver Latin writers commonly shortened final -*o* (cf. 13b), irrespective of the quantity of the preceding syllable—e.g. *sermŏ,* which is obviously not a case of *brevis brevians,* and could never be scanned thus in Plautus.] As an aid to scansion, throughout this work syllables shortened by *brevis brevians* are *always* specially marked as short, as in the Plautine line quoted above.

15. *Elision and hiatus.* The following rules govern the conditions in which a vowel concluding a word is directly followed by another vowel beginning the next word.

Elision. Normally a final vowel, or a vowel +*m*, is suppressed or *elided* before another vowel (or *h*) beginning the next word:

e.g. conticuer(e) omnes intentiqu(e) ora tenebant.

                                                (V. *Aen.* ii.1)

monstr(um) horrend(um) inform(e) ingens cui lumen
ademptum   (*Aen.* iii.658)

This practice is extremely common in the colloquial verse of comedy, common also in Virgil, notably less so in later dactylic and lyric poets. A few times Virgil even elides between line and line ('hypermetric elision', nearly always of -*que*), e.g. *Georg.* ii.344–5.

si non tanta quies iret frigusque caloremqu(e)
inter,

and similar elision is very occasionally found in other hexameter poets, and in Horatian lyrics where there is strict *synaphea* (**19**), e.g. *Odes* iii.29.35–6.

[In Virgil and other stricter dactylic poets, however, it is rare for a long final vowel to be elided before a short syllable, and almost unknown before the second short syllable of a dactyl — ᵛ ᵛ.]

27

Prodelision. The same process is said to occur in reverse ('prodelision' or 'aphaeresis') with the word *est*, which loses its *e* after a final vowel or *m* (e.g. *usa (e)st*), or—in early Latin—after -*ŭs* and -*ĭs* (e.g. *opust = opus (e)st*).

Hiatus. A final vowel (or *m*) standing *unelided* before another vowel is said to be in *hiatus*. *Hiatus* is common in Homer, and consequently we find it used by Virgil as an affectation in lines bearing other traces of Grecisms (13c, 74), e.g.

> stant et iuniperī } et castaneāē } hirsutae[1]   (*Ecl.* 7.53)
> Glaucō } et Panopeāē } et Inoo Melicertae.   (*Georg.* i.437)

the final diphthong of *Panopeae* in the second example being shortened by the process known as correption (again common in Homer).

Except for such 'Grecisms', hiatus is not common in the stricter dactylic and lyric poets; but it occurs freely in the colloquial verse of comedy, especially at certain points in the line (cf. **43B, 44B, 48B, 53B**). [Indeed, in scenic poetry long open monosyllables (e.g. *qui*) are shortened in hiatus no less often than they are elided: but such hiatus is restricted to the *first* half of a double-short element—i.e. *ān quĭ* } *ămānt* is correct, *ānnĕ quĭ* } *ādsunt* incorrect.]

Basic rhythms

16. Rhythm is constituted by the build-up of 'short' and 'long' elements (as described above) into various regular patterns. The following are the basic rhythmical units used in Latin verse:

> ⏓ — ⏑ —   Iambic metron. [Single iambus = ⏑ —[2]]
> — ⏑ — ⏓   Trochaic metron. [Single trochee = — ⏑[2]]
> ⏑⏑ — ⏑⏑ —   Anapaestic metron. [Single anapaest = ⏑⏑ —[2]]
> — ⏑⏑   Dactyl.

---

[1] The sign } is used throughout this work to denote any syllable in hiatus; when it is absent, it may be assumed that elision takes place, and future cases of elision will *not* be specially marked by parenthesised letters. Cf. Introductory Note.

[2] These single 'feet' are *not* units of movement: cf. **17.**

$-\smile-$ Cretic.

$\smile--$ Bacchius.

$\smile\smile--$ Ionic.

$-\smile\smile-$ Choriamb.

The following 'feet' are found as ingredients in lines based on the above rhythms, but are not in themselves the basis of any rhythm:

$\smile\smile$	Pyrrhic.	$--\smile$	Palimbacchius.
$--$	Spondee.	$-\smile\smile\smile$	First paeon.
$\smile\smile\smile$	Tribrach.	$\smile\smile\smile-$	Fourth paeon.
$\smile\smile\smile\smile$	Proceleusmatic.	$---$	Molossus.

17. *Foot and metron.* The term *metron* is used to denote the irreducible unit of movement in any given rhythm, and terms such as dimeter, trimeter, tetrameter indicate the number of such units contained in a line: thus a trochaic dimeter consists of two trochaic metra as defined above, $-\smile-\overset{\smile}{-} \mid -\smile-\overset{\smile}{-}$. The term *catalexis* indicates that a line is docked of its final element: thus a trochaic dimeter catalectic $= -\smile-\overset{\smile}{-} \mid -\smile-$.

A *foot* is not necessarily a unit of movement, although in many cases the foot is incidentally the equivalent of the metron: thus in the dactylic hexameter one can speak almost indifferently of feet and metra. But (as implied in **16**) in iambic, trochaic and anapaestic verse the metron unit consists of *two* 'feet'; and, in these rhythms, although sub-division into feet may be helpful for schematic purposes or to illustrate principles of word-division, it must never be forgotten that the single foot is *not* a unit of movement. Cf. footnote to **34A**.

18. *Caesura and diaeresis.* These terms are used to indicate division between words within a line; word-division within a foot or metron is called *caesura*, word-division at the end of a foot or metron *diaeresis*. (But there is no genuine 'break' before the 'enclitic' word *est*, or after 'proclitic' prepositions such as *ab*, *in*.)

19. *Final anceps; synaphea.* In most metrical structures, the end of a line is marked not only by word-division but by a certain indifference to the quantity of the final syllable. Thus in the iambic trimeter

$$\cup - \cup - \quad \cup - \cup - \quad \cup - \cup -$$

the final long element may be represented by a short syllable, as in

tuo stetisse dicit in cacuminĕ   (Cat. 4.16)

and often at the end of the dactylic hexameter, and of the iambic lines of dramatic dialogue. A short syllable in such a position is sometimes known as *brevis in longo*, or the last element may be referred to as 'final *anceps*'; and 'doubtful' elements of this type even occur from time to time at the midpoint of certain longer lines in Plautus and Horace (cf. **43–4B, 48B, 53B, 94, 95**).

There are, however, certain lyric metres in which final *anceps* (or hiatus between lines) is rarely or never tolerated, and there is strict metrical continuity between, as well as within, lines. This continuity is termed *synaphea*; it prevails, notably, in the alcaic and sapphic stanzas (**139, 141**) of Horace, *Odes* iv (i–iii are slightly less strict in this respect), and in Seneca's anapaests (**100**). Thus at Sen. *Med.* 99–100

vilia currant, placet in vulnūs $- \cup \cup - - \quad \cup \cup - - -$
maxima cervix $- \cup \cup - -$

the final syllable of *vulnus* is not a *brevis in longo*, but is regularly lengthened by the opening *m* of *maxima*, as though the two words occurred in the same line. (Cf. **13**.) Synaphea may even be emphasised by 'hypermetric' elision (**15**) between lines, e.g.

saltuumque reconditor(um) $- \cup - \cup \cup - \cup -$
amniumque sonantum $- \cup - \cup \cup - -$
          (Cat. 34.11–12)

—a licence which is even found occasionally in dactylic hexameter verse.

CHAPTER 3

Word-Accent; Saturnian Verse; the Influence of Accent throughout Latin Verse Literature

Significance of word-accent in Latin verse

20. As stated in the previous chapter (**11**), although rhythm in classical Latin verse is measured basically by the principles of quantity, there are nevertheless indications that word-accent was of far more importance to the Latin than to the Greek poets.

One reason for this may be that the Latin language (as compared with Greek) is very rich in quantitatively 'long' syllables —a fact which probably contributed to the Latin tendency towards a stronger word-accent. The literary consequences of this are as follows and are considered in turn later in this chapter:

(a) it is at least arguable, and is widely believed, that the primitive form of Latin verse known as 'saturnian' was based on principles of accent rather than those of quantity (cf. **22–25**).

(b) even when quantitative scansion had been established (largely, perhaps, through literary Greek influence), the classical Roman poets showed a considerable regard for the influence of word-accent (cf. **26–27**).

(c) after the classical period, accent became by degrees the determining factor in mediaeval Latin verse, of which Italian is the natural descendant (cf. **28**).

It is in fact possible (if perhaps dangerous) to regard the Greek influence as having produced an episode of quantitative verse-writing in the history of a language more naturally tending towards accentual scansion. [For *ictus* cf **12ⁿ**.]

Principles of accent

21. Put briefly, the principles of word-accent in classical Latin[1] are as follows: the accent falls

(a) on the first syllable of dissyllabic words: e.g. *móntes, áquae.*

(b) in words of more than two syllables, on the penultimate syllable if this syllable is long: e.g. *magíster, magistrŏrum*; but otherwise on the ante-penultimate syllable, e.g. *dóminus, móntĭbus, iúdĭces.*

[(c) it is generally thought that longer words, with two or more syllables preceding the primary accent, may have been given a secondary accent, e.g. *labòriósus, ìnsonuérunt*—but this may not have been present when the primary accent was preceded only by two *short* syllables, as in *mĕdĭtáris.*]

(d) where an enclitic (*-que, -ne* or *-ve*) is added to a word, it is usually stated that the accent shifts if necessary: thus *bélla— béllaque,* but *móntes—montésque.* [But there is some uncertainty concerning the normal practice in cases such as *lúmina— lumínaque* or *lúminàque?* Nor is it certain what rule was followed when the suffix was elided: *montésqu(e)* or (perhaps more probably) *móntesqu(e)*?]

Exceptions to these rules are rare and will not be noted here.

ACCENT IN THE HISTORY OF LATIN LITERATURE

Saturnian verse

22. In a work of this nature, there is no space for a full discussion of saturnian verse: not only is the subject outstandingly problematical, but the ancient literature involved is scanty, fragmentary and unlikely to be widely read by students. But a brief statement of the subject is necessary, both for the sake of completeness and as part of the progressive history of accent in Latin verse.

The saturnian metre is mainly important as being almost the only form of verse which at least *may* have evolved before Greek quantitative principles exerted their influence on Roman

[1 In very early Latin it is sometimes held that the accent fell on the first syllable of most words.]

poetry. Saturnians are used most notably by the epic poets
Livius Andronicus and Naevius (3rd century B.C.), and also
occur in early inscriptions, epitaphs and prophecies. In the last
instances, however, much additional doubt can be cast by the
question of what does, and what does not, constitute a saturnian;
and even in the epic poems, attempts to force the line into a
scheme have led to unnecessary emendations.

23. Almost the only undisputed fact about the saturnian line is
that it falls into two segments, separated in nearly every case by
word-division; and that hiatus (**15**) is tolerated at the midpoint[1]
(at least) of the line, as in the opening of Livius' *Odyssia*:

> virum mihi, Camena, |} insece versutum.

But the length of the two segments varies considerably: a total
of 13 syllables to the line is regular, but there are lines with as
few as 11, or as many (perhaps) as 18 syllables—though here
further uncertainty is caused by questions of elision and hiatus
(**15**). And, as will shortly be seen, this variety in length cannot
be explained by 'normal' principles of resolution, or the
equation $- = {\smile}{\smile}$.

[A further feature in some saturnian lines is alliteration within or between the segments: this can be seen in *v*irum and
*v*ersutum in the above example, or in Naevius'

	magnae *m*etus tumultus	*p*ectora *p*ossidit
and	superbiter *c*ontemptim	*c*onterit legiones.

But this feature is also common enough in other early Latin
verse, and is unlikely to have any particular structural significance in this case.]

24. *Quantitative theory of scansion.* It has been fashionable since
ancient times to consider the 'normal' saturnian length as
exemplified by

> malum dabunt Metelli | Naevio poetae
>
> (Metelli, *fr.* 1B)

[1 A characteristic of certain dialogue metres in Roman comedy, and
found even in lyric: cf. 43-4B, 48B, 53B, 95, 106-7, 114, 119.]

This verse can be scanned quantitatively as two iambic-trochaic segments, of seven and six syllables respectively

$$\cup - \cup - \quad \cup - - \mid - \cup - \cup - - \quad \text{(cf. 44A, 55A)[1]}$$

and the combination has been likened to the nursery-rhyme distich

> The queen was in her parlour
> Eating bread and honey.

But the pitfalls of such scansion are demonstrated by the following typical instances, at least when they are scanned by familiar rules of quantity:

(LIVIUS, *Odyssia*)			
virum mihi, Camena, }	insece versutum	∪ — ∪ — ∪ — —	— ∪ ∪ — — —
tuque mihi narrato }	omnia disertim	— ∪ ∪ — — — —	— ∪ ∪ ∪ — —
in Pylum devenies	aut ubi ommentans	— ∪ — — ∪ ∪ —	— ∪ ($\stackrel{\smile}{-}$) — — —
atque escas habemus	mentionem	— (∪) — — ∪ — ∪ —	— ∪ — —
(NAEVIUS, *Bellum Poenicum*)			
noctu Troiad exibant	capitibus opertis	— — — ∪ — — —	∪ ∪ ∪ ∪ — —
multi alii ex Troia	strenui viri	— (—) ∪ ∪ (—) — — —	— ∪ — ∪ —
senex fretus pietati	deum allocutus	∪ — — — ∪ ∪ —	∪ (∪) — ∪ — —
inerant signa expressa	quomodo Titani	∪ ∪ — — (∪) — — —	— ∪ — — — —
Runcus atque Purpureus	filii Terras	— ∪ — ∪ — ∪ ∪ —	— ∪ — — —
prima incedit Cereris	Proserpina Puer	— (∪) — — — ∪ ∪ —	— — ∪ ∪ ∪ —
deinde pollens sagittis	inclutus arquitenens	— ∪ — — ∪ —	— ∪ ∪ — ∪ ∪ —
sanctus Iove prognatus	Putius Apollo	— — ∪ ∪ — —	— ∪ ∪ ∪ — —
superbiter contemptim	conterit legiones	∪ — ∪ — — —	— ∪ — ∪ ∪ — —

Many of these examples can only be forced into the quantitative scheme by abandoning the 'classical' rules and postulating *ad hoc* principles of quantity and elision/hiatus, and by arbitrary emendation. At the best, it must be admitted that if saturnians were indeed composed on a theory of quantity, that theory is but distantly related to the quantitative rules of the classical period.

25. *Accentual theory of scansion.* Recent scholars have inclined to the belief[2] that saturnians were composed on a principle of word-accent in which quantity had not yet achieved import-

---

[1 And attempts have been made to derive this form from a Greek compound known as 'archilochean dicolon'.
'Ερασμονίδη Χαρίλαε, χρῆμά τοι γελοῖον ⏓ — ⏒ — ⏒ — ⏑ | — ∪ — ∪ — —]
[2 Encouraged by a statement (admittedly disputable) of the ancient critic Servius.]

ance: so that the 'normal' line quoted in **24** was conceived as málum dábunt Metélli | Naévio poétae.

Perhaps the most popular view is that saturnian verses contained five principal accents, three in the first segment and two in the second—as in the last example—and that unaccented syllables were relatively unimportant, though kept *roughly* within limits by the natural principles of accentuation (**21**). This theory is not without its drawbacks: as already stated (**21ⁿ**), the actual rules for word-accent in early Latin are not universally agreed, and the question of secondary (as well as primary) accent is sometimes disputed[1]. But application even of the 'normal' rules for accentuation produces a system that at least seems more coherent and flowing than quantitative scansion. So much can be seen from a reiteration of previous examples:

vírum	míhi,	Cam|éna, }		ínsece	ver|sútum
túque	míhi	narr|áto }		ómnia	dis|értim
átque	éscas	hab|émus		mènti	ónem
nóctu	Tróiad	ex|íbant	{ cap|ítibus[2]	op|értis
			cápitibus	
múlti	álii	ex Tróia	strénui	víri
sénex	frétus	piet|áti	déum	alloc|útus
ínerant	sígna	ex|préssa	quómodo	Tit|áni
Rúncus	átque	Pur|púreus	fílii	Térras
príma	in|cédit	Céreris	Pro|sérpina	púer
deínde	póllens	{ sag|íttis[2]	ínclutus	ar|quítenens
		ságittis	
sánctus	Ióve	prog|nátus	Pútius	Ap|óllo[3]

[The above theory does not explain *all* saturnian lines satisfactorily, e.g.

supérbiter contémptim   cónterit legiónes

or   bicórpores Gigántes   mágnique Atlántes

which appear to fall short of the norm by one accent; and a slight refinement, not without its attractions, is to this effect: that the line concludes with *four* 'vital' accents (two in each segment), but that the first of these may be preceded by a vari-

[1] Earlier supporters of the accentual theory held that the second segment, as well as the first, contained three accents—i.e. Naévió poétae.]

[2] The accentual problem of these words can merely be indicated here.]

[3] There may also be some significance in the actual length of words in the saturnian line—at all events, it is remarkable how many surviving saturnians conform to the type $2 + 2 + 3/3 + 3$ *sanctus*| *Iove* | *prognatus* ¦ *Putius* | *Apollo.*

35

able number of 'preparatory' syllables—whether accented or not—thus:

malum	dábunt	Met|élli		Naévio	po|étae
virum	míhi,	Cam|éna, }		ínsece	ver|sútum
in	Pýlum	de|vénies		aút ubi	om|méntans
inerant	sígna	ex|préssa		quómodo	Ti|táni
su	pérbiter	con|témptim		cónterit	legi|ónes
bi	córpores	Gi|gántes		mágnique	At|lántes

This refinement admittedly helps to account for some saturnians which otherwise seem of intractable length, and a roughly analogous principle may perhaps be seen in the 'reciting notes' opening plainsong chants.]

Accent in the 'classical' period

26. Even after quantitative verse was established in Latin literature, word-accent played an important secondary rôle. As stated above, one reason for this may lie in the language's natural richness in quantitatively long syllables, which the Roman poets also involuntarily counteracted by the following practices *not* directly connected with accentuation:

(a) frequent disappearance (for the purposes of quantity) of final -*s* in early Latin verse: e.g. *omnibu' rebus.* (Cf. **13c.**)

(b) regular shortening of final -*o* (except in dative/ablative singular) in post-Augustan verse: e.g. *sérmŏ.* (Cf. **13b**: this licence is also found in earlier verse with certain words, notably *egŏ*, where it can be seen as an application of the accentual law of *brevis brevians* below, **26d**—but here it is extended far beyond those bounds.)

(c) the marked tendency to shorten 'doubtful' syllables, except in the most studied imitations of Greek practice. (e.g. *pătres* preferred to *pātres*: cf. **13d**.)

But in the following instances it will be seen that word-accent *does* play an important part in counteracting this richness in naturally long syllables:

(d) the law of *brevis brevians* (**14**), by which, in 'colloquial' verse, a long syllable is shortened by a preceding short syllable, *so long as* it is also directly preceded *or* followed by a syllable

36

with word-accent: e.g. *vídēn tu* becoming *vídĕn tu*, *vŏlūptátem* becoming *vŏlŭptátem*.

(e) in the iambic and trochaic verse of early drama, the large proportion of spondaic feet, which are admitted even at places where they are not found in Greek verse—e.g. the second foot of the iambic metron, which allows $\overset{\scriptscriptstyle\vee}{-} - \vee -$ in Greek, and in the stricter verse of other Latin poets (e.g. Horace) but $\overset{\scriptscriptstyle\vee}{-} - \overset{\scriptscriptstyle\vee}{-} -$ in Republican drama (cf. further 30B). But here it is *highly* significant that a spondee in this position *rarely* involves word-accent on the originally short element marked in heavy type above: i.e.

is leno, ut se aequom (e)st, *flócci nón* fecit fidem.

$$-- \quad -- \mid -\acute{-}-\acute{-} \mid ---\vee- \qquad \text{(Pl. } Rud. \text{ 47)}$$

is regular, whereas the following would be irregular:

is leno, ut se aequom (e)st, *nón flócci* fecit fidem.[1]

$$-- \quad -- \mid -\acute{-}\acute{-}- \mid ---\vee-$$

27. Finally, there is probably considerable significance in certain principles of word-division in Latin verse, which (especially in and after the Augustan period) are observed far more strictly than in the Greek poets. This is shown, for example, by the 'rules' for caesura and line-ending in hexameter and elegiac verse (cf. **66ff.**, **83ff.**), and in Horatian alcaics (cf. **141**). Not all these rules can, or need, be explained solely by considerations of word-accent; but (to take one instance) it is a fact—whether regarded as the source or the consequence of such principles— that in the 'regular' Virgilian hexameter, word-accent must *coincide* with the opening syllables of the last two feet, and *conflicts* at least once, and usually more often, in the centre of the line. Thus the most 'normal' type of Virgilian line, with 'strong' third foot caesura, shows no coincidence in the centre of the line:

Títyre, | tú pátul|ae récub|ans sub | tégmine | fági (*Ecl.* 1.1)

while in the case of the 'weak' caesura (far rarer than in Greek hexameters) there is coincidence in the third foot, but not in the second or fourth:

formós|am reson|áre dóc|es Amar|ýllida | sílvas (*Ecl.* 1.5)

[1 Except in certain circumstances. Cf. **38B**, **49B** for a more precise formulation of this 'rule'.]

and in both instances the rules for line-ending ensure coincidence in the last two feet.

Accent in mediaeval Latin verse

28. 'Classical' merges into 'mediaeval' Latin with a gentleness which defies rigid dividing-lines. The subject of mediaeval Latin verse is outside the scope of this work; but, in the context of this chapter, it must be realised that in the 'mediaeval' period accent gradually superseded quantity as a basis for rhythm, the language thus producing the models for accentual verse in English and other 'modern' languages.

Of the classical metres, only the 'iambic' $\overset{\smile}{-} - \smile -$ and the 'trochaic' $- \smile - \overset{\smile}{-}$ (cf. Ch. 4) lent themselves easily to accentual scansion; and the process described above was an uneven one. Thus the same period of writing (roughly mid-5th century A.D.) could produce two stanzas as quantitatively different as the following examples, whose rhythm is nevertheless basically the same:

(a) a sólis órtus cárdine $- \acute{-} \smile \acute{-}$ $- \acute{-} \smile -$
adúsque térrae límitem $\smile \acute{-} \smile \acute{-}$ $- \acute{-} \smile -$
Chrístum canámus príncipem $\acute{-} - \smile \acute{-}$ $- \acute{-} \smile -$
nátum María vírgine. $\acute{-} - \smile \acute{-}$ $- \acute{-} \smile -$

(b) maíor et énim sólito $\left[\acute{-} \smile \smile \acute{\smile} \right.$ $- \acute{\smile} \smile - \left. \right]$
appàruísti}ómnibus $- \acute{-} \smile \acute{-}$ $\overset{\smile}{-} \acute{-} \smile -$
ut pòtestátis órdinem $- \acute{\smile} - \acute{-}$ $\smile \acute{-} \smile -$
inlústri ménte vínceres. $\left. - \acute{-} - \acute{-} \right.$ $\smile \acute{-} \smile \acute{-}$

The first example can be scanned on purely quantitative principles as a stanza of iambic dimeters (**40A**); the second can *only* be scanned accentually, the quantity symbols producing no coherent pattern. Trochaic verse adapts itself even more readily to accentual scansion: this may be seen from the famous mediaeval hymn

díes írae, díes ílla

or from another late example of much the same date (13th century), where again quantity symbols are meaningless:

(c) véni, sáncte spíritus,
    ét emítte caélitus
    lúcis túae rádium;
    véni, páter paúperum,
    véni, dátor múnerum,
    véni, lúmen córdium.

In rhyme[1] as well as rhythm this hymn looks forward to the modern English style embodied, for example, in its familiar translation by J. M. Neale:

> Come, thou holy paraclete,
> And from thy celestial seat
> Send thy light and brilliancy;
> Father of the poor, draw near:
> Giver of all gifts, be here:
> Come, the soul's true radiancy.

[1 Rhyme itself played no structural part in Latin verse of the classical period, although Roman poets of many types made *occasional* and effective use of assonance. That close assonance *except* for effect was regarded as a blemish in serious verse is perhaps indicated by the rarity of 'jingles' in dactylic poetry; but an exception is found in the dactylic pentameter (78ff.) whose two 'halves' rhyme quite frequently, as in

flammaqu(e) in argut*o* saepe reperta for*o*   (Ov. *Ars Amatoria* i.80)

In mediaeval Latin, rhyme gradually became common: its foreshadowing of modern style is well shown by the hymn quoted above. And rhyming devices came to be affected even in strictly 'quantitative' verse, as in the mediaeval species of hexameter known as 'leonine'; a term which covers not only simple rhyme between centre and end of line

(e.g. martyr sancta d*ei*, quae flagrans igne fid*ei*)

but also more complicated rhyming devices both within *and* between lines, as in

hora novissima, tempora pessima sunt, vigilemus.
ecce minaciter imminet arbiter ille supremus.

or   Stella maris, quae sola paris sine coniuge prolem,
iustitiae clarum specie super omnia solem,
gemma decens, rosa nata recens, perfecta decore,
mella cavis inclusa favis imitata sapore.]

39

CHAPTER 4

Iambic and Trochaic Verse

29. The iambic movement ᵕ—ᵕ— ... and the trochaic
—ᵕ—ᵛ ... have an obvious similarity in themselves, and this
similarity is borne out by the actual use of the rhythms in
Latin (as in Greek) verse. For this reason, it is convenient to
consider the two movements within the same chapter.

There is, however, a striking difference between two types:

  (**A**) the sophisticated use of these rhythms by the Roman lyric
    poets and Seneca, following on the whole the Greek
    pattern; and

  (**B**) the less strict rules of the early Roman dramatists and a
    few later imitators (notably Phaedrus).

For the sake of clarity, these two types are (as far as possible)
considered separately in the following pages: the left-hand page
of each pair describes the general principle of any given line together with its 'type **A**' use, while licences and divergences
peculiar to 'type **B**' are treated in parallel on the right-hand
page.

(This distinction in treatment is employed, however, for
purely practical purposes, and should not be taken as implying
that the two types are *really* distinct in principle, or that 'type **B**'
need be regarded as deriving, in origin, from 'type **A**'.)

41

A

Iambic and trochaic metron—'type A'

30A. As stated in **17**, in these rhythms the metron (i.e. the basic unit of movement) consists of *two* feet: thus (basically) the iambic metron = ◡ — ◡ —, the trochaic = — ◡ — ◡. But the *first* short element of the iambic metron, and the *second* of the trochaic, can be lengthened, thus giving ◡͞ — ◡ — and — ◡ — ◡͞, the variable element being called *anceps*.

In addition, in both rhythms long syllables are occasionally resolved into double-short, ◡͞ ◡◡ ◡ ◡◡ and ◡◡ ◡ ◡◡ ◡͞ ; and in certain conditions this licence of resolution is even extended to the *anceps*, giving such forms of metron as ◠ — ◡ — and — ◡ — ◠. This last licence is, however, more restricted in the 'Grecising' verse now being considered than in the freer verse of 'type B' (see opposite page).

B

Iambic and trochaic metron—'type B'

30B. The iambic and trochaic metra of the early Roman dramatists, and their imitators, differ from the type described on the opposite page in the following respects:

(1) within certain limits, *both* the short elements of the metron can be lengthened, thus giving ⌣̄ — ⌣̄ — (iambic) and — ⌣̄ — ⌣̄ (trochaic).

(2) resolution of long syllables is far commoner than in 'type A', and *anceps* syllables are also freely resolved, so that the full scheme of the iambic metron becomes ⏑⏑ ⏑⏑ ⏑⏑ ⏑⏑, and that of the trochaic ⏑⏑ ⏑⏑ ⏑⏑ ⏑⏑.

In this type of verse, identification and scansion are often comparatively difficult, owing to

(i) the variety in forms of metron possible.

(ii) the high frequency of elision (**15**), especially in Plautus and Terence.

(iii) unfamiliar differences in quantity produced by the *brevis brevians* law (**14**). (As an aid to scansion, in the succeeding sections syllables certainly shortened[1] by *brevis brevians* are specially marked as such, thus: *volŭptatis.*)

[In general, the two types of verse run so much after one pattern that it is sometimes helpful to conceive of both (as the poets unquestionably did) merely as alternations of *anceps* and long elements ... × — × — × — × ... from which segments can be cut, the use of the terms 'iambic' and 'trochaic' depending only on whether a segment begins with *anceps* or long. There are certain features common to both metres, and obviously identical, whose nature is obscured if we speak too rigidly in

[1 There are many instances where the shortening is possible but *not* certain—either because an *anceps* element is involved, or because of the possibility of synizesis (**13**), e.g. Pl. *Rud.* 650—

quis istic est, qui deŏs tam parvi   ⌣⌣⌣ — —   ⌣⌣ — — — —

or   quis istic est, qui deôs tam parvi   ⌣⌣⌣ — —   — — — — ?]

43

B

terms of iambic and trochaic 'feet'. Thus the following state-
ments apply to both metres:

(a) resolved *anceps* readily precedes but very seldom follows
resolved long (cf. further **32B**, **47B**). (In terms of 'feet' we
should say that the proceleusmatic foot is common in iambic
verse, ⌣̆⌣ ⌣̄⌣, but very rare in trochaic, ⌣̄⌣ ⌣̆⌣, while a tribrach or
dactyl foot followed by an anapaest is common in trochaic verse
but very rare in iambic.)

(b) there is a strong tendency for word-accent (**21**) to coincide with the first syllable of a resolved *long* element, and *not*
to fall on the syllable immediately preceding or following this
point—i.e. ₓ⌣̄⌣́ is regular, ⌣́⌣̄⌣ and ₓ⌣̄⌣́ are avoided. Largely related to this is the rarity (discernible also in 'type A' verse) with
which word-division occurs within such a resolved element.
Cf. **38B**, **49B** for further details.

(c) a resolved *anceps* may not be followed, or divided in the
middle, by the end of a word spilling over from the preceding
long. (The 'law of the split anapaest', which, in the sequence
— ⌣̈⌣ —, excludes *corde ⋮ volunt* and *cordibus ⋮ hunc*, but admits
cor ⋮ quod ⋮ amat, cor ⋮ dolet ⋮ huic, and, of course, *cordolium*.)

(d) certain principles of word-division are shared by the
iambic senarius (**32B**), with the trochaic septenarius (**47B**),
which indeed may be seen as a senarius with an extra three
elements at the beginning, as indicated by the following scheme:

iamb. sen.   × — × — × — × — × — ⌣ —
troch. sept.   — × — × — × — ×₁— × —₂× —₃⌣ —

For (i) in both lengths, there is usually a central word-division
after an *anceps* element (most frequently at the point marked ₁
in the above scheme)[1]; (ii) in both, a spondaic or anapaestic
word or word-end,. . . ⌣̄⌣ —, very seldom concludes at the point
marked ₂ unless the remainder of the line, from ₂ onwards, is
covered by a single word (as in the ending *abduxi ⋮ negotiis* or

[1]The use of the term caesura or diaeresis (cf. **18**) depends merely on
whether one happens to be counting in iambic or trochaic feet. For details
cf. **36B**, **48B**.]

A

INDIVIDUAL IAMBIC AND TROCHAIC
LENGTHS FOUND IN LATIN LITERATURE

IAMBIC

The iambic trimeter

32A. As the name implies, this line consists of three iambic metra of the type described in **30A**, though with certain restrictions. It is extremely common in Greek literature, being

↓
B

nequitiem ⋮ *patefeceris*) (cf. **38B, 49B**); (iii) in both, an iambic
word or word-end, . . . ᵛ —, may not conclude at the point
marked ₃ (cf. **32B, 47B**).]

31B. *Nomenclature.* The 'type B' licences just described make the
separate 'feet' of each metron virtually identical; hence it has
become common for the foot, rather than the two-foot metron,
to be regarded as the unit of movement, and names are given to
'type B' lines on this principle. Thus the trimeter of 'type A'
(signifying three metra) is rechristened 'senarius' (signifying six
feet) in 'type B', and similarly the tetrameter ('type A') is rechristened 'octonarius' ('type B').

It must be emphasised, however, that even in 'type B' the two-
foot metron remains the real unit, since lines consisting of an odd
number of feet do not occur. [The term 'septenarius' is particularly misleading in this respect—cf. **44B**.]

[*Restrictions of word-accent.* A further distinction is imposed by
considerations of word-accent, whose importance in Latin verse
was described in **20ff**. It is very significant that, when the
central short syllable of the metron is lengthened under the
'type B' licence (᷉ — — — iambic or — — — ᷉ trochaic), that
syllable *very rarely* coincides with a word-accent. (Cf. **26e**, and
38B, 49B for the effect of this restriction on various individual
lines.]

INDIVIDUAL IAMBIC AND TROCHAIC
LENGTHS FOUND IN LATIN LITERATURE

IAMBIC

Iambic senarius

32B. The iambic senarius is an extremely common dialogue-
metre of early Roman drama, and is most familiar in the
comedies of Plautus and Terence. It admits the following

employed (as is well known) for most of the dialogue of Greek tragedy, e.g. Eur. *Medea* 1–2

εἴθ' ὤφελ' 'Αργοῦς μὴ διαπτάσθαι σκάφος
Κόλχων ἐς αἶαν κυανέας Συμπληγάδας

— — ◡ —   — — ◡ —   — — ◡ —

— — ◡ —   — ◡◡ ◡ —   — — ◡ —

In Latin (as in Greek) literature, when this line is used repeatedly there is no 'synaphea' (19)—i.e. the last syllable of the line can be left short, or (if a vowel) in hiatus (15), as between the two lines of the following example—Cat. 29.3–4.

Mamurram habere quod comata Gallia
habebat uncti et ultima[1] Britannia

◡ — ◡ —   ◡ — ◡ —   ◡ — ◡◡[2]

33A. *'Pure' iambic trimeter.* Very occasionally, series of trimeters are found built entirely on the 'pure' metron ◡ — ◡ —, without variation, as in the last example, or in

phaselus ille, quem videtis, hospites,
ait fuisse navium celerrimus

◡ — ◡ —   ◡ — ◡ —   ◡ — ◡ —   (Cat. 4.1–2)

['Pure' trimeters of this type alternate with dactylic hexameters in H. *Epod.* 16: cf. 92.]

34A. *'Normal' lyric iambic trimeter.* More usually, lyric iambic trimeters admit the following variations:

(a) long *anceps* (making a spondaic foot[3]) at the beginning of a metron: e.g. H. *Epod.* 17.53–5.

[1] For the lengthening in this position of the final syllable of *ultima*, cf. 13d.]
[2] The concluding syllables of these lines are in fact examples of 'final *anceps*' (19). Future cases of such 'final *anceps*' will be treated as long syllables.
[3] This is the conventional way of putting the matter. But the use of such terms is dangerous unless it is clearly realised that, in iambic and trochaic verse, apparently spondaic or dactylic or anapaestic 'feet' are merely accidental combinations of syllables, and have nothing to do with true dactylic and anapaestic verse; and, likewise, that the 'foot' is not a unit of movement in itself, though it can be a useful subdivision for scansional purposes. Cf. 17.

48

B

variations, most of which distinguish it unmistakably from the
trimeter of 'type A':

(a) long *anceps*, making in effect a spondaic foot − − to replace the iambus ˅ −. Such spondees are exceedingly common,
and can occur in *any* foot of the line except the last, which is invariably an iambus.

(i) In the first, third and fifth feet they are found as freely as
in 'type A' trimeters, e.g. Ter. *H.T.* 9.
existumarem scire vostrum, id dicerem.
− − ˅ −   − − ˅ −   − − ˅ −

[In fact the *fifth* foot does not often remain a 'pure' iambus, as
in *H.T.* 14

quantum ille potuit cogitare commode
− − ˅ ͡˅   − − ˅ −   ˅ − ˅ −

and *must not* be a pure iambus if it is followed by word-division
(i.e. if the sixth foot consists of a separate iambic word). A line
such as the following is thus exceptional (though readily explained, in this instance, by the close connection of its final
words):

sed dextrovorsum avorsa it in mălām ⋮ crŭcem
(Pl. *Rud.* 176)

The only notable relaxation of this rule is found when word-
division occurs within, as well as after, the fifth foot, as in

nunc mi opportuna hic esset, salvă ⋮ sī ⋮ fŏret.
(*Rud.* 802)

and in such cases the monosyllable closing the fifth foot (i.e. *si* in
the above example) goes more closely with the following than
the preceding word.

The general tendency towards a spondaic fifth foot is still
more pronounced in the 'type A' trimeters of Seneca, where the
iambus in this position is almost unknown (cf. **35A**).]

A

quid obseratis auribus fundis preces?
non saxa nudis surdiora navitis
Neptunus alto tundit hibernus salo.

॒ — ॒ —   — — ॒ —   — — ॒ —

— — ॒ —   — — ॒ —   .॒ — ॒ —

— — ॒ —   — — ॒ —   — — ॒ —

[Roman writers showed a distinct aversion (derivable from the
early Greek lyric poets) from ending a trimeter with two consecutive iambic *words*; thus an ending such as

capaciores adfer huc, ⋮ puer, ⋮ scyphos

॒ — ॒ —   — — ॒ —   ⋮ ॒ — ⋮ ॒ —   (*H. Epod.* 9.33)

is exceptional. A very similar aversion can be seen in the 'type B'
trimeter—cf. **32B** (a)(i).]

(b) resolution of long syllables, giving in effect a dactyl
— ⏗ or a tribrach ॒ ⏗ in the first foot of a metron, or a tribrach
in the second foot of a metron (except at the end of the line):

*deripe*re lunam vocibus possim meis

— ⏗ ॒ —   — — ॒ —   — — ॒ —   (H. *Epod.* 17.78)

[But such resolution is uncommon in 'golden age' writers, and
the following line is exceptional in this respect:

*aliti*bus at*que canibus homi*cidam Hectorem

— ⏗ ॒ —   ॒ ⏗ ॒ ⏗   — — ॒ —   (H. *Epod.* 17.12)]

[(c) resolution of long *anceps*, giving an anapaestic foot—
again, an effect very rare in the Augustan age, e.g.

*pavidum*que leporem et advenam *laqueo* gruem

⏗ — ॒ ⏗   ॒ — ॒ —   ⏗ — ॒ —   (H. *Epod.* 2.35)]

35A. *Iambic trimeter of silver Latin writers.* As used by Seneca (in
his tragedies), and by other 'silver Latin' writers such as
Petronius and Martial, the iambic trimeter shows the following
developments:

(a) the fifth foot of the line is *very rarely* an iambus: here long
anceps predominates, as in Sen. *Med.* 1

di coniugales tuque gen*ialis* tori

— — ॒ —   — — ॒ ॒॒   — — ॒ —

B

(ii) spondees are also very common in the second and fourth feet[1], e.g. Ter. *H.T.* 1

nequoi sit vostrum mirum, quor partis seni

‿ ‿ ‿ ‿   ‿ ‿ ‿ ‿   ‿ ‿ ⏑ ‿

[But cf. 38B for certain restrictions on word-division and word-accent in this instance.]

(b) resolution of long syllables into double-short, giving in effect a dactyl — ꙮ or tribrach ⏑ ꙮ in any foot of the line except the last: e.g. Ter. *H.T.* 420–2

aut ego profecto *ingenio egregio ad mise*rias
natus sum, aut illud falsumst, quod volgo audio
dici, *diem adi*mere aegritud*inem homi*nibus.

(c) resolution of the lengthened *anceps*, giving an anapaest ꙮ —, again common in any foot of the line except the last: e.g. Ter. *H.T.*

477 *minumo* periclo id demus adulescentulo.

ꙮ ‿ ⏑ ‿   ‿ ‿ ⏑ ꙮ   ‿ ‿ ⏑ ‿

481 quantam fenestram ad ne*quitiem patefe*ceris

‿ ‿ ⏑ ‿   ‿ ‿ ꙮ ‿   ꙮ ‿ ⏑ ‿

483 nam det*erio*res omnes sum*ŭs* licentia

‿ ‿ ꙮ ‿   ‿ ‿ ‿ ꙮ   ⏑ ‿ ⏑ ‿

(d) resolution of anceps and long syllable in the same foot,

[1 The admission of the spondee in these places produces much the most startling divergence from the Greek pattern. The *anapaest* is very common in all feet, except the last, of the Greek *comic* trimeter, e.g. (to take an extreme case) Aristoph. *Vespae* 979

κατάβα, κατάβα, κατάβα, κατάβα, —καταβήσομαι.

⏑⏑‿⏑⏑‿   ⏑⏑‿⏑⏑‿   ⏑⏑‿⏑‿

and even the proceleusmatic foot ꙮ ꙮ is found in Menander, though not in Aristophanes; but the licence of a second- or fourth-foot spondee is unknown in Greek.]

51

A

[an iambic fifth foot is fairly rare in the 'type B' senarius
(cf. **33B**); but its rarity is still more pronounced in the present
instance.]

(b) resolved feet are common, as in the above example, and
in

    atram cruen*tis manib*us amplexae facem
    ades*te, thala*mis horridae quondam meis

    — — ᴗ —   — ⌣ ᴗ —   — — ᴗ —
    ᴗ — ᴗ ⌣   — — ᴗ —   — — ᴗ —   (*Med.* 15–16)

(c) in particular, the long *anceps* is often resolved, giving an
anapaestic foot. Such anapaestic feet are not confined (as in
Greek tragedy) to the opening of the verse, as in

    *taciti*sque praebens conscium sacris iubar
    ⌣ — ᴗ —   — — ᴗ —   — — ᴗ —   (*Med.* 6)

but are especially common in the third metron (i.e. as the fifth
foot), e.g.

    hoc restat unum, pronubam *thalamo* feram
    ut ipsa pinum postque sac*rificas* preces

    — — ᴗ —   — — ᴗ —   ⌣ — ᴗ —
    ᴗ — ᴗ —   — — ᴗ —   ⌣ — ᴗ —   (*Med.* 37–8)

[(d) Very rarely, a 'proceleusmatic' foot ⌣ ⌣ (such as is
common in 'type B' verse, cf. **35B**d) is produced at the beginning of the line by the resolution of the opening *anceps and* the
succeeding long syllable: e.g.

    *pavet ani*mus, horret, magna pernicies adest.
    ⌣ ⌣ ᴗ —   — — ᴗ —   ⌣ — ᴗ —   (*Med.* 670)]

36A. *Caesura.* In all the forms of iambic trimeter outlined above,
there is regularly word-division (caesura, **18**) after the first
syllable of the third foot, as in

    crinem solutis ⫶ squalidae serpentibus
    — — ᴗ —   — ⫶ — ᴗ —   — — ᴗ —   (*Med.* 14)

or (less frequently) of the fourth foot, e.g.

    exul pavens invisus ⫶ incerti laris
    — — ᴗ —   — — ᴗ ⫶ —   — — ᴗ —   (*Med.* 21)

(Greek iambic trimeters are subject to the same caesura 'rule'.)

↓
B

producing the 'proceleusmatic' ⌣⌣ : this is most commonly
found at the opening of the line, e.g. Ter.*H.T.* 100

    *neque ut ani*mum decuit aegrotum adulescentuli

    ⏖ ⏖ — ⏖ ⏑ — — ⏖ — — ⏑ —

but it occurs occasionally in any foot except the last—e.g. Pl.
Rud. 462

    satin nequam sum, ut *pote qui hodie* amare inceperim?

    ⏖ — — — ⏖ ⏖ ⏑ — — — ⏑ —

[Although the resolved feet, as listed above, are common
enough in themselves, it is exceedingly rare (as mentioned in
30B) for a resolved long element to be directly *followed* by a resolved anceps: therefore—in iambic verse—the sequence dactyl
or tribrach + anapaest or proceleusmatic hardly occurs.]

36B. *Caesura.* There is regularly word-division (caesura, **18**)
    (a) after the first syllable of the third foot, e.g. Pl. *Rud.* 75

        de navi timidae ⦙ desiluerunt in scapham.

        — — — ⏖ — ⦙ — ⏖ — — — ⏑ —

and/or (b) (less frequently) after the first syllable of the fourth
foot, e.g. *Rud.* 80

        adulescens huc iam adveniet ⦙ quem videbitis

        ⏖ — — — — ⏖ — ⦙ — ⏑ — ⏑ —

Alternatively, an elision (**15**) *before* the third or fourth foot is

A

[**37A.** '*Porson's law*'. A familiar restriction in Greek iambic trimeters is that a spondaic fifth foot may *not* be broken by caesura
(Porson's 'law of the final cretic'.) This 'law' is not observed in
Greek *comedy*, nor in the 'free' Latin iambics of 'type B' (see
opposite page); of the 'type A' iambics under discussion, it may
be noticed that

(a) Horace does *not* strictly observe this law[1], which is not
infrequently broken by such lines as
    neque ut superni villa cand*ens* T*us*culi

    ◡ — ◡ —   — — ◡ —   — : — ◡ —   (H. *Epod.* 1.29)

(b) In Seneca, where a spondaic fifth foot is especially common (cf. **35A**), 'Porson's law' *is* strictly observed; but an elision
(**15**) at this point is clearly regarded as permissible. Thus there
are many examples of the type
(*Med.* 22)   iam notus hospes limen ali*en*(*um*) *ex*petat

    — — ◡ —   — — ◡ ⌣̑   — : — ◡ —

while endings such as the following (without such elision) are
extremely rare
(*H.F.* 255)   natos paterni cadere reg*ni vi*ndices

    — — ◡ —   — ⌣̑ ◡ —   — : — ◡ —]

[**38A.** *Word-division within resolved elements.* The double-short of
resolved elements is very rarely 'broken' by word-division: thus
in Sen. *Med.* 1

        di coniugales tu*qu*⸍   *gen*ialis tori
        — — ◡ —   — — ◡ : ⌣̑   — — ◡ —

division follows the *first* syllable of the tribrach, while division

[[1] *except* in *Epode* 17 (the only poem in which he uses the trimeter in
unvaried series), where he conforms to the Senecan restrictions, cf. b.]

54

B

regarded as equivalent to a caesura within it: e.g. Ter. *H.T.* 66

ita ăttente tut(e) ⋮ illor(um) ⋮ officia fungere.

$\frown$ — — — ⋮ — — ⋮ — $\frown$ ᴗ — ᴗ —

[37B. *'Porson's law'*. The restriction known as 'Porson's law' (cf. 37A on opposite page) is not enforced in this type of verse.]

[38B. *Word-division and accent.* The following additional points of word-division deserve attention, and are also illustrative of the Roman regard for word-accent (cf. 20ff.):

(a) a spondaic or anapaestic word (or word-end) very seldom forms the second foot of a metron—i.e. the second or fourth foot of the senarius: thus a line such as

et vos a vost | ris ab*duxi* | rebus, patres

is generally avoided. This rule indicates a certain regard for the second *anceps* of the iambic metron (which of course is invariably short in 'type A' verse—cf. 30A), and its effect is that a

55

A

after the *second* syllable would split the resolved element, and is thus avoided. The principle behind this restriction is probably at least partly one of word-accent, as is still clearer from the analogous rules governing 'type B' verse (cf. **38B** on opposite page).

At the beginning of a line, however, it is permissible for an opening anapaest to be 'broken' by word-division, as in Sen. *Med.* 43

    et ⁞ *inhos*pitalem Caucasum mente indue

↓
B

lengthened or resolved *anceps* at this point very rarely coincides with word-accent. Exceptionally, this word-division may occur after the fourth foot of the senarius if the remaining dipody of the line is covered by a single word, as in

et vos a vost | ris abdúxi | negótiis   (Pl. *Rud.* 89)

which incidentally ensures that in that dipody accent will fall on a long element and not an *anceps*.[1]

(b) in the case of resolved feet, there are certain principles of word-division which are partly attributable to Greek influence, but which are largely intensified by word-accent. The strong tendency is for word-accent to coincide with the beginning of the resolved element in the tribrach and dactyl of iambic verse (i.e. ⏕ ⏖), or in the second part of the proceleusmatic (⏑⏑⏖); and it is notably rare for this point to be *immediately* preceded or followed by accent. Largely for this reason, word-division seldom occurs *within* the resolved element: for such division produces an accentual clash. Most frequently word-division *precedes* the resolved element. Similarly, an 'iambic' foot may not be formed by a self-contained dactylic or tribrach word (e.g. *córpŏrĕ, lătĕrĕ*), except at the beginning of the line, where a *dactylic* word is occasionally found, as in

omnibus amicis . . . .[2]

(c) the resolved *anceps* of anapaest ⏖ — (and proceleusmatic ⏖⏑⏑) may not be followed, nor split in the middle, by the end of a word spilling over from the preceding foot. (The 'law of the split anapaest'.)

This law is thus satisfied by Ter. *H.T.* 474

consilia ad adulescentis; et ┊ *tibi* ┊ *per*dere

---

[1] This restriction is shared with trochaic verse—cf. **49B**, and for the general principle **30B**. For a similar restriction in cretic verse, cf. **116ⁿ.**]

[2] The rule against self-contained dactyls is not broken when the foot is followed by elision, since here the accent falls correctly on the beginning of the resolved element, as in Ter. *H.T.* 420

aut ego profect(o) *ingéni(o) egrégi(o)* ad miserias.

For rules governing dactylic and tribrach words in anapaestic verse, cf. **106ⁿ.**]

A

39A. The full scheme of the 'type A' trimeter is thus as follows:

Metra	I			II			III		
Feet	1	2		3	4		5		6

(a) *In Catullus and Horace*
Iambi ᴜ — ᴜ — ᴜ ∣ — ᴜ ∣ — ᴜ — ᴜ ˰
Spondees — — — — ∣ — — —
Tribrachs ᴜᴜᴜ ᴜᴜᴜ ᴜ ∣ ᴜᴜ ᴜ ∣ ᴜᴜ
Dactyls — ᴜᴜ — ∣ ᴜᴜ
Anapaests (ᴜᴜ —)

(b) *In Seneca and Petronius*
Iambi ᴜ — ᴜ — ᴜ ∣ — ᴜ ∣ — (ᴜ—) ᴜ ˰
Spondees — — — — ∣ —
Tribrachs ᴜ ᷇ ᴜ ᷇ ᴜ ∣ ᷇ ᴜ ∣ ᷇
Dactyls — ᷇ — ∣ ᷇
Anapaests ᴜᴜ —
Proceleusmatics (᷇ ᷇)

Other iambic lengths

40A. *Iambic dimeter.* Iambic lengths of two metra ('dimeters'), built on the same principle as trimeters, make occasional appearances in Latin lyric. Scheme: ˰ — ᴜ — ˰ — ᴜ —, with occasional resolutions: but resolved feet are notably rare in Horace.

Sometimes unvaried series of these dimeters are found, e.g. Sen. *Ag.* 759ff.

instant sorores squalidae	— — ᴜ —	— — ᴜ —
sanguinea iactant verbera,	— ᷇ ᴜ —	— — ᴜ —
fert laeva semustas faces	— — ᴜ —	— — ᴜ —
turgentque pallentes genae.	— — ᴜ —	— — ᴜ —

B

but would be broken by

      consilia ad adulescentis; per*dere* ⁞ *sed* tibi.

All the rules noted in this section have their counterparts in trochaic verse—cf. **49B**. And for the essential similarity in these respects between iambic and trochaic the reader is referred especially to **30B**.]

39B. The full scheme of the 'type B' senarius is thus as follows:

Metra	(I)		(II)		(III)	
Feet	1	2	3	4	5	6
Iambi and spondees	⏓ —	⏓ —	⏓	— ⏓	—	⏓ — ⏑ ⏔
Tribrachs and dactyls	⏓ ⏑⏑	⏓ ⏑⏑	⏓	⏑⏑ ⏓	⏑⏑	⏓ ⏑⏑
Anapaests and proceleusmatics	⏑⏑ ⏑⏑	⏑⏑ ⏑⏑	⏑⏑	⏑⏑ ⏑⏑	⏑⏑	⏑⏑ ⏑⏑

Other iambic lengths

40B. *Iambic quaternarius.* The iambic dimeter of 'type A' has its 'type B' counterpart in the quaternarius, a line of four iambic feet which makes occasional appearances in Roman comedy. It admits the following variations:

(a) long *anceps* (i.e. spondee — — replacing iambus ⏑ —) in any foot except the last, which is always a 'pure' iambus: basic scheme ⏓ — ⏓ — ⏓ — ⏑ —, varied by

(b) resolutions: tribrach ⏑ ⏔, dactyl — ⏔ and anapaest ⏔ — all admitted in the first three feet [the same principles of word-division being observed as in the senarius, **38B**].

59

and *Aus.* ii.2.1–2

    puer eia surge et calceos   ⏓ — ∪ —   — — ∪ —
    et linteam da sindonem.   — — ∪ —   — — ∪ —

More commonly, dimeters are found alternating with other lines—e.g. with dactylic lengths, as in H. *Epod.* 14–15 (cf. **92a**; and cf. also **94–95** for *Epod.* 11 and 13).

41A. *Iambic trimeter—dimeter combinations.* Particularly common is the couplet form where a trimeter is followed by a dimeter: this is the metre of Horace's first ten epodes, and it is also used by Martial and Ausonius, and in the *Appendix Vergiliana.*
exx. (a) beatus ille, qui procul negotiis,
       ut prisca gens mortalium,
       paterna rura bubus exercet suis,
       solutus omni faenore.

    ∪ — ∪ —   ∪ — ∪ —   ∪ — ∪ —

    — — ∪ —   — — ∪ —

    ∪ — ∪ —   ∪ — ∪ —   — — ∪ —

    ∪ — ∪ —   — — ∪ —   (H. *Epod.* 2.1–4)

  (b) (with occasional resolution)
       has inter epulas ut iuvat pastas ovis
       videre properantis domum.

    — — ∪ ⏓   — — ∪ —   — — ∪ —

    ∪ — ∪ ⏓   — — ∪ —   (H. *Epod.* 2.61–2)

[Such resolution is much rarer in the dimeter than the trimeter: indeed, Horace furnishes only one other example.]
  (c) Later use—anapaests admitted at the opening of either length, and in the third metron of the trimeter (cf. **35Ac**):
       procul horridus Liburnus et querulus cliens,
       imperia viduarum procul.

    ⏓ — ∪ —   ∪ — ∪ —   ⏓ — ∪ —

    — ⏓ ∪ ⏓   — — ∪ —   (Mart. i.69.33–4)

42A. *The scazon.* The scazon, or 'choliambus' (= 'limping iambus') is an iambic trimeter with a dragged or 'limping' close

↓
B

e.g. Pl. *Pseud.* 204–6

nimium stultus, nimium fui ⌒ — — — ⌒ — ˘ —
indoctus; illine audeant — — ˘ — — — ˘ —
id facere quibus ut serviant — ⌒ ˘ ⌒ — — ˘ —

Occasionally short 'systems' of these quaternarii are found, as in the foregoing example; in general, the line is rare, although a single quaternarius is sometimes found among longer iambic lengths such as the 'octonarius', in whose structure it is closely concerned: cf. next section.

(For the use of the quaternarius in the *versus reizianus*, cf. **46B**.)

—the final foot must be a spondee. Adopted from the work of Greek poets (e.g. Hipponax) by Varro and others, it is used by Catullus in a number of poems, e.g.

> miser Catulle, desinas ineptire,
> et quod vides perisse perditum ducas;
> fulsere quondam candidi tibi soles.

$\breve{\underline{}} - \smile - \quad \breve{\underline{}} - \smile - \quad \smile - - -$ (Cat. 8.1–3)

As indicated by the above examples, the fifth foot is always a pure iambus from the time of Catullus onwards, presumably to emphasise—or to compensate for—the dragged close. [This restriction is not observed by the Greek poets, nor in the earlier Latin scazon of Varro.]

(a) In Catullus the full 'scheme' of the line is

$$\breve{\underline{}} \,(\overline{\smile\smile})\, {}^{\smile}(\overline{\smile\smile})\, \breve{\underline{}} \mid (\overline{\smile\smile})\, {}^{\smile} \mid - \smile - - -$$

—as indicated, the resolved feet are only rarely found, e.g.

> quem non in aliqua re videre Suffenum

$- - \smile \widehat{\smile\smile} \quad - - \smile - \quad \smile - - -$ (Cat. 22.19)

(b) In later use of the scazon (by Persius, Martial and Ausonius) the resolved feet occur more often, and the anapaest is admitted at the opening of the line, so that the full 'scheme' becomes

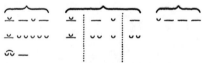

e.g. dederas, Apici, bis trecenties ventri,
et adhuc supererat centies tibi laxum.

$\smile\smile - \smile -\!- \quad - - \smile - \quad \smile - - -$

$\smile\smile -\!- \smile\smile \quad -\!- - \smile -\!- \quad \smile - - -$ (Mart. iii.22.1–2)

B

43B. *Iambic octonarius.* This eight-foot iambic line has no counter-part in 'type A' Latin verse, although it is clearly descended from the iambic tetrameters of Greek satyr-plays such as Sophocles' *Ichneutae*, e.g.

μὴ νῦν ἀπίστει, πιστὰ γάρ σε προσγελᾶ θεᾶς ἔπη

(*Ichn.* 291)

63

B

As a dialogue metre, it makes occasional appearances in
Plautus and Terence; as in the senarius, under certain conditions (see below) the iambus ᴗ— is freely replaced by spondee
— —, tribrach ᴗ⁓, dactyl —⁓, anapaest ⁓— or (rather
rarely) proceleusmatic ⁓⁓[1]; but the final foot of the line is
always a pure iambus. e.g. Pl. *Pseud.* 149–52:

> verum ita vos estis neglegentes, perditi, ingenio improbo,
> officium vostrum ut vos malo cogatis commonerier,
> nempe ita animati } esti' vos; vinciti' duritia hoc atque me,
> hoc sis vide, ut alias res agunt! hoc agite, hoc animum
>   advortite.

```
— ⁓ — —    — — ᴗ —    — — ᴗ —    ⁓ — ᴗ —
— ⁓ — —    — — ᴗ —    — — — —    ᴗ — ᴗ —
— ⁓ ᴗ —    ᴗ — ᴗ —    — ⁓ — ⁓    — — ᴗ —
— — ⁓ ⁓    — — ᴗ —    — ⁓ — ⁓    — — ᴗ —
```

[Two somewhat differing varieties of this line should be distinguished.
(a) when there is word-division (diaeresis, **18**) after the
fourth foot, the line falls naturally into two equal halves, and
gives the impression of two unlinked quaternarii of the type described above, **40B**. This impression is increased by the following additional restrictions:

  (i) in this variety, the fourth foot (as well as the eighth) is
  always a pure iambus, so that the scheme of the line is

```
᷃  ᴗᴗ  ᷃ᴗᴗ  ᷃ᴗᴗ  ᴗ ᴗ | ᷃  ᴗᴗ  ᷃ᴗᴗ  ᷃ᴗᴗ  ᴗ ᴗ
```

  (ii) as implied by the above scheme, the last syllable of the
  fourth foot (preceding the diaeresis) may be shortened
  like a final *anceps*, as in Pl. *Poen.* 819

> is me autem porro verberat, | incursat pugnis, calcibus.

```
— —    — —    — — ᴗ ᴗ |   — — — —    — — ᴗ —
```

and in Plautus though not in Terence, this syllable may

[1 *Word-division in resolved feet.* The same rules apply as in the senarius—
cf. **38B**.]

65

A

44A. *Catalexis in iambics.* Occasionally in iambic verse (as in trochaic and other types), a syllable is suppressed in the concluding metron of a line. This process is called 'catalexis', and a line with such suppression is called 'catalectic', e.g.

(a) *catalectic dimeter.* (ᴗᴗ) — ᴗ —   ᴗ — —

This line is very rarely found, but is used in series by Petronius, e.g.

> Horatium videmus,
> versus tenoris huius
> nusquam locasse iuges   (Petr. *fr.* 18B.1–3)

66

↓
B

even end in an unelided final vowel, left in hiatus (**15**),
e.g. Pl. *Pseud.* 191

mihi ĕt familiae omni sit meae, }⋮ atque adeo ut
frumento affluam

⌒⌒ ∪—   —‿∪— ⋮ —⌒—— ——∪—

Poen. 818

studeo hunc lenonem perdere, }⋮ ut meum erum
miserum macerat

⌒— —— ——∪⩒ ⋮ —⌒ —⌒ ——∪—

(b) when there is no diaeresis after the fourth foot, word-
division (caesura, **18**) usually occurs instead in the fifth foot. In
this instance, the fourth foot need *not* be a pure iambus, but is
granted the same licences as the other feet, so that the scheme of
the line is

⨯̆ ⩒ ⨯̆ ⩒ ⨯̆ ⩒ ⨯̆ ⩒ ⨯̆ ⋮ ⩒ ⨯̆ ⩒ ⨯̆ ⩒ ∪ —

This variety is much commoner than the other in Terence,
e.g. *H.T.* 185–6

quam vellem Menedemum invitatum, ut nobiscum esset,
amplius

ut hanc laetitiam necopinanti primus obicerem ē͡i domi!

—— —⌒ ———— —⋮——— ∪—∪—

∪— —⌒ —⌒—— —⋮—∪⌒ ∪—∪—]

A

In one lyric of Seneca (*Med.* 849–78) systems of such lines are closed with a still more shortened clausula, e.g. 855–7

        quatiens superba motu   ◡◡—◡— ◡——

        regi minatur ultro,   ——◡— ◡——

        quis credat exulem?   ——◡— ◡—

[For the catalectic dimeter's *apparent* part in saturnian verse, cf. 24.]

(b) *catalectic trimeter.* ⏓—◡(◡◡) ⏓—◡— ◡——

e.g.   trahuntque siccas machinae carinas   (H. *Od.* i.4.2)

This line occurs in two odes of Horace (i.4 and ii.18), in each case alternating with another length—cf. **54A, 55A, 96.**

(c) *catalectic tetrameter.* ⏓—◡— ◡—◡— ⏓—◡— ◡——

e.g.   remitte pallium mihi meum, quod involasti (Cat. 25.6)

This line is used (unvaried) in one poem (25) of Catullus; the 'pure' iambic foot predominates—in striking contrast to the 'heavy' use of the line in 'type B' verse, where it is commonly called 'septenarius' (see opposite page).

↓
B

44B. *Iambic septenarius.* This line is the counterpart of the 'type A' catalectic tetrameter (see opposite page). [The name septenarius is misleading, since the line does not consist of seven feet, but of eight with 'catalexis' —i.e. lacking a final syllable. Cf. 30B.]

This line is clearly descended from the catalectic tetrameter of Greek comedy, e.g. Aristoph. *Ranae* 907–8

καὶ μὴν ἐμαυτὸν μέν γε τὴν ποίησιν οἷός εἰμι,
ἐν τοῖσιν ὑστάτοις φράσω, τοῦτον δὲ πρῶτ' ἐλέγξω.

It is much commoner in Roman comedy than the octonarius described in **43B**. As in the senarius, the iambus ◡ — is freely replaced by spondee — —, tribrach ◡ ⌢, dactyl — ⌢, anapaest ⌢ — and (rather rarely) proceleusmatic ⌢ ⌢[1].

[For restrictions on the fourth foot, cf. below, (a).]

Even the seventh foot is not *bound* (as it is in Greek tetrameters) to be a pure iambus, as will be seen from the final line of the following example (Pl. *Rud.* 324–8)

vale.—valete. credidi: factum est quod suspicabar,
data verba ero sunt, leno abit scelestus exulatum,
in navem ascendit, mulieres avexit: hariolus sum.
is huc erum etiam ad prandium vocavit, sceleri' semen.

[1 *Word-division in resolved feet.* The same rules apply as in the senarius— cf. **38B**.]

↓

A

[*Apparent departures from the metron-scheme. The alcaic nine-syllable*
45A. It is only seldom that iambic lines are found which do not
divide evenly into two-foot metra (with or without 'catalexis',
44A).

B

nunc quid mihi meliust, quam ilico his opperiar erŭm dum
   veniat?

⏑ —   ⏑ —   ⏑ —   ⏑ —   — —   ⏑ —   ⏑ — —

◠ —   ⏑ —   — —   ⏑ —   ⏑ —   ⏑ —   ⏑ — —

— —   — —   — ◠   ⏑ —   — —   ⏑ ◠   ⏑ — —

⏑ —   ⏑ ◠   — —   ⏑ —   ⏑ —   — ◠   ⏑ — —

— —   ◠ ◠   — —   ⏑ —   — ◠   ⏑ ◠   — ◠ —

There is normally word-division (diaeresis, **18**) after the
fourth foot. This is almost invariable in Plautus, and in this case
the fourth foot *must* be a pure iambus, as in all the lines of the
above example, so that the true scheme is

   ⏓⏖   ⏓⏖   ⏓⏖   ⏑ — ┆ ⏓⏖   ⏓⏖   ⏓⏖ —

And, as implied by the above scheme, the last syllable of the
fourth foot (preceding the diaeresis) may be shortened like a
final *anceps*, as in Pl. *Rud.* 321

   cum istiŭs modi virtutibus ┆ operisque natus qui sit

   — ◠ ⏑ —   — — ⏑ ⏓ ┆ ◠ — ⏑ —   — — —

or (in Plautus though not in Terence) left unelided in hiatus, as
in *Rud.* 329

   eadem, sacerdos Veneria } ┆ haec si quid amplius scit.

   ◠ —   ⏑ —   — ◠ ⏑ ⏓ ┆ — — ⏑ —   ⏑ — —

[On a few occasions (only) in Terence there is *no* diaeresis after
the fourth foot. In this case there is usually word-division
(caesura, **18**) in the fifth foot, and the fourth foot need *not* be a
pure iambus—e.g. *Hec.* 254

   aut ea refellendo aut purgando ┆ vobis corrigemus

   — ◠   ⏑ —   — — — —   — ┆ — — —   ⏑ — —

(For an analogous—and much commoner—variety of octonarius, cf. **43**Bb.]

[*Apparent departures from the metron-scheme*

45B. As observed in **30B**, it is only rarely that iambic lines are
found (even in this type of verse) which do not divide evenly
into two-foot metra, with or without 'catalexis' (**44A**).

A

The most notable exception is found in the alcaic stanza of Horace and his imitators. The ingredients of this stanza are chiefly aeolic (cf. **141**), but the third line appears to be the equivalent of an iambic dimeter with an extra syllable, i.e. (basically) $\smile - \smile - \quad \smile - \smile - \smile$. In practice, the opening syllable of the line is usually, and the central syllable always, long, as in

si fractus illabatur orbis

$- - \smile - \quad - - \smile - -$ (H. *Od.* iii.3.7)

For a full description of this line, and of the stanza in general, cf. **141**.]

B

An exception may perhaps be seen in the length ⏑ — ⏑ — — (the equivalent of 2½ iambic feet) which is sometimes found at the end of a series of bacchii (⏑ — — . . .); for this length cf. **113b.** And it may be significant that this length is one variant form of the reizianum, which is next to be described.]

46B. *Reizianum and versus reizianus.* In Greek lyric verse, the name reizianum is given to the short aeolic form ⏓ — ⏑ ⏑ — —, which is often found in tragic chorus among other aeolic lengths, and also occurs repeatedly in the anonymous 'swallow song' (*fr.* 32 D²)

ἦλθ' ἦλθε χελιδών,
καλᾰ̆ς ὥρᾱς ἄγουσα.

(For the place of this line in aeolic verse, cf. **131e, 135.**)
The name *versus reizianus* is given to the combination where this length follows an iambic dimeter, as at Aristoph. *Acharnenses* 840–1

ἢ συκοφάντης ἄλλος, οἰ-	— — ⏑ — — — ⏑ —
μώζων καθεδεῖται.	— — ⏑ ⏑ — —

In Latin verse, the reizianum seems to shed much of its aeolic affinity, both because of its constant association with iambic verse and because of the great variety of forms to which it can run. Its full scheme in Plautus seems to be

⏓ ⏖ ⏓ ⏖ —

and almost as many variants are admitted as in the first 2½ feet of the iambic senarius—to which (under this scheme) it has a clear similarity—e.g.

iam noscere possis[1]	(*Pl. Aul.* 441)	— — ⏑ ⏑ — —
focum si adesses	(*Aul.* 439)	⏑ — ⏑ — —
merito id tibi factum est	(*Aul.* 440)	⏑ ⏑ — ⏑ ⏑ — —
quid comminatus?	(*Aul.* 421)	— — ⏑ — —
quid, stolide, clamas?	(*Aul.* 415)	— ⏑ ⏑ ⏑ — —

[¹ It should, however, be noticed that this line would *not* make an admissible iambic segment owing to the principle of the 'split anapaest'—cf. **38B.**]

A

TROCHAIC

Trochaic tetrameter 'catalectic'

47A. As the name implies, this line consists of four trochaic metra of the form described in **30A**, the last metron being 'catalectic', or lacking a syllable:

It is said to have been the original metre of Greek tragic dialogue, and is found not infrequently in surviving Greek tragedy, e.g. Aesch. *Persae* 155–6

ὦ βαθυζώνων ἄνασσα Περσίδων ὑπερτάτη,

μῆτερ ἡ Ξέρξου γεραιά, χαῖρε, Δαρείου γύναι

Adopted (like the iambic trimeter) by the Roman poets, it makes occasional appearances in Latin literature of the type under consideration, though much commoner is its 'type B' use described on the opposite page under the title 'septenarius'.

74

↓
B

nos coquere hic cenam (*Aul.* 431, 435) — ‿‿ — — —
tibi secŭs quam velles? (*Aul.* 436) ‿‿‿‿ — — —

In Roman comedy the reizianum makes occasional appearances in unvaried systems, or among other metres: but much its commonest association is with the iambic quaternarius (**40B**), to which it is repeatedly linked to form the Latin counterpart of the *versus reizianus* illustrated above: thus at Pl. *Aul.* 439–43

ibi ubi tibi erat negotium, ad focum si adesses,
non fissile auferres caput: merito id tibi factum est,
adeo ut tu meăm sententiam iam noscere possis:
si ad ianuam huc accesseris, nisi iusserŏ, propius
ego te faciam miserrimus mortalis uti sis.

⌢⌢ ‿ —   ‿ — ‿ —   ‿ — ‿ — —
— — ‿ —   — — ‿ —   ‿‿ — ‿‿ — —
⌢ — — ⌢   — — ‿ —   — — ‿‿ — —
— — ‿ —   — — ‿ —   ‿‿ — ‿‿‿‿ —
⌢ — ⌢ —   ‿ — ‿ —   — — ‿‿ — —

Cf. also **142**.

TROCHAIC

Trochaic septenarius

47B. This line is the counterpart of the 'type A' catalectic tetrameter (see opposite page). As in the case of the iambic septenarius, the name is misleading, since the line consists not of seven feet, but of eight with 'catalexis'—i.e. lacking a·final syllable, cf. **44A**.

The septenarius is a very common dialogue metre in early Roman drama (often, though by no means always, in scenes of excitement), and admits the following variations, most of which distinguish it unmistakably from the tetrameter of 'type A':

(a) long *anceps*, making in effect a spondaic foot — — to replace the trochee — ‿. Such spondees are very common, and can occur anywhere in the line except in the last complete foot (i.e. the seventh).

A

The following licences (akin to those of the iambic trimeter, cf. **34A**) add variety to the line:

(a) Long *anceps* (making a spondaic foot[1]) at the end of a metron: e.g. *Pervigilium Veneris* 1

cras amet qui numquam amavit, quique amavit cras amet.

— ∪ — —   — ∪ — —   — ∪ — —   — ∪ —

[The *anceps* of the sixth foot is always so lengthened in Seneca—cf. **35A**.]

(b) Resolution of long syllables, making in effect a tribrach ⌒ ∪ in any foot, and an anapaest ⌒ — in place of a spondee to end a metron: e.g. Sen. *Phaedr.* 1207–8

tuque semper, *genitor*, irae *facilis* assensor meae,
morte *facili* dignus haud sum qui nova natum nece

— ∪ — —   ⌒ ∪ — —   ⌒ ∪ — —   — ∪ —
— ∪ ⌒ —   — ∪ — —   — ∪ — —   — ∪ —

[But such resolution is rare towards the end of the line.]

(c) Resolution of the lengthened *anceps*, giving in effect a dactylic foot — ⌒. This resolution (practically excluded from Greek trochaics) is found occasionally in the second foot of the line, and with surprising freedom in the sixth foot, e.g.

ac repente sancta fontis lympha *Castali*i stetit.

— ∪ — —   — ∪ — —   — ∪ — ⌒   — ∪ —   (Sen. *Oed.* 229)

gravior uni poena sedeat coniug*is soce*ro mei.

⌒ ∪ — —   — ∪ ⌒ —   — ∪ — ⌒   — ∪ —   (Sen. *Med.* 746)

[This licence may be compared with the later Roman poets' very similar admission of an anapaest in the fifth foot of the iambic trimeter, which gives in effect the same ending to the line—cf. **35Ac**.]

---

[1] Cf. footnote to **34A**.

↓
B

(i) in the second, fourth and sixth feet they are found as freely as in the 'type A' tetrameter, e.g. Pl. *Rud.* 741
immo Athenis natus altusque educatusque Atticis.

    — ◡ — —   — ◡ — —   — ◡ — —   — ◡ —

[In fact, the sixth foot seldom remains a 'pure' trochee, as in Pl. *Rud.* 738
nam altera haec est nata Athenis ingenuis parentibus

    — ◡ — —   — ◡ — —   — ⌢ — ◡   — ◡ —

and *must not* be a 'pure' trochee if there is word-division (caesura, **18**) within both the sixth and seventh feet. Thus *Rud.* 775 is exceptional:
quaere erum atque adduce.—at hic ne . . .—maximo
⋮ malo ⋮ suo

    — ◡ — —   — ◡ — —   — ◡ — ⋮ ◡   — ⋮ ◡ —

This restriction (and the general tendency towards a spondaic sixth foot) has an exact analogy in the rules for the *fifth* foot of the iambic senarius, which ends with the same syllabic sequence—cf. **32B**.]

(ii) spondees are also very common in the first, third and fifth feet, e.g. *Rud.* 715
nive in carcerem compingi te est aequom aetatemque ibi

    — — — ◡   — — — —   — — — —   — ◡ —

[But cf. **49B** for certain restrictions on word-division and word-accent in this instance.]

(b) resolution of long syllables into double-short, giving in effect a tribrach ⌢◡ as a substitute for the trochee, and an anapaest ⌢ — as substitute for the spondee: e.g. *Rud.* 619–20
*statui*te exemplum impudenti, *date pu*dori praemium,
facite hic lege *potius liceat* quam vi victo vivere.

    ⌢ ◡ — —   — ◡ — —   ⌢ ◡ — —   — ◡ —

    ⌢ — — ◡   ⌢ — ⌢ —   — — — —   — ◡ —

(c) resolution of the lengthened *anceps*, giving a dactyl — ⌢ in any of the first six feet: e.g. *Rud.* 615–16
pro Cyrenen*ses popula*res, vostram ego imploro fidem,

77

A

[48A. *Diaeresis.* There is regular word-division (diaeresis, 18) after the fourth foot of the line—e.g. after *fontis* and *sedeat* in the preceding examples.

The Greek poets' avoidance of word-division after a spondaic second or sixth foot is not followed in Latin trochaics. (Compare the Roman poets' indifference to 'Porson's law' in the iambic trimeter—cf. 37A.)]

[49A. *Word-division within resolved elements.* As in the case of iambic verse of this type (cf. 38A), word-division is not permitted to break up resolved elements. Thus the tribrach of trochaic verse may be broken after the second syllable ($\widehat{\smile\smile}$ | $\smile$) but not after the first ($\smile$ | $\smile\smile$).]

↓
B

agricolae, accolae propinqui qui estis *his regi*onibus.

— —   — —   — ᷟ — —   — ᴗ   — —   — ᴗ —

ᷟ ᴗ   — ᴗ   — ᴗ — —   — ᴗ   — ᷟ   — ᴗ —

[But the dactyl is not common in the fourth foot, for reasons given in **49B**.]

[(d) resolution of long syllable and *anceps* in the same foot, producing the 'proceleusmatic' ᷟ ᷟ : this foot must occasionally be acknowledged, but is very rare in trochaic verse, for reasons given in **30B**.]

[**48B**. *Diaeresis*. There is usually **word-division** (diaeresis, **18**) after the fourth foot, as in all the foregoing examples, e.g. after *populares* and *propinqui* in **47B**c.

In lines without such diaeresis, word-division regularly occurs within the fourth foot (and/or after the fifth), as in Pl. *Poen.* 505
praesertim homini amanti, qui ⁞ quicquid agit ⁞ properat omnia

— —   ᷟ ᴗ   — —   — ⁞ —   ᷟ —   ⁞ ᷟ ᴗ   — ᴗ   —

In the verse of Plautus (but not that of Terence), it is not uncommon for hiatus (**15**) to occur at the central break in the line[1], e.g. *Rud.* 636
  et tibi eventuram hoc anno } ⁞ uberem messem mali

— ᴗ — —   — — — —   ⁞   — ᴗ — —   — ᴗ —]

[**49B**. *Word-division and accent*. Attention is drawn to certain additional principles of word-division and accent, which have their exact analogies in iambic verse (cf. **38B**; and, for a broad treatment of these principles as they affect both iambic and trochaic verse, the reader is referred especially to **30B**):

(a) a caesura *within* the second, fourth or sixth foot of the trochaic septenarius is seldom preceded by a spondaic or anapaestic word or word-end: thus a line such as the following is generally avoided—
  fraudis sceleris parricidi per*iuri* ⁞ plenus, pater

[1 Or at a change of speaker; cf. **43B**, **44B** for hiatus within longer *iambic* lines, and **106–7** for the same licence in anapaests.]

↓
B

This rule indicates a certain regard for the *anceps* elements of the first, third and fifth feet (which of course are always short in 'type A' verse—cf. 30A); and its effect is that a lengthened *anceps* at any of these points very rarely coincides with word-accent. Exceptionally, this rule may be broken in the fifth and sixth feet when the remainder of the line is covered by a single word, as at Pl. *Rud.* 651

> fraudis sceleris parricidi peri*ú*ri ⦙ plen*í*ssimus

—an effect which incidentally ensures that in that word accent falls on a long element and not on an *anceps*.

(b) in the case of the tribrach and anapaest (⌢ ᵛ and ⌢ —), there is a strong tendency for word-accent to coincide with the beginning of the resolved element, $\underset{\times}{\acute{\frown}}$; and it is rare for this point to be *immediately* preceded or followed by accent. Largely for this reason, word-division often occurs directly after (and not within) these feet, as in Pl. *Rud.* 770

> teque ambustulatum ob*iciam* ⦙ magnis *avibus* ⦙ pabulum

—and division is rare within the resolved element. Similarly, a tribrach or anapaestic foot may not begin with the second syllable of a dactylic or tribrach word—an effect which would produce an accentual clash (e.g. *cór*|*p̑ŏr̆e̯*, *lát*|*ĕr̯ĕ*).

(c) in the dactylic foot — ⌢, the resolved *anceps* may not be divided or split, unless it is *also* preceded, by word-division: thus

> multa fert lub*íd*(o) :⦙ *ĕă* ⦙ facere prohibet tua praesentia

(Ter. *H.T.* 573) is admissible, but the rule would be broken by

> multa fecit: *plūrĭmă* ⦙ facere prohibet tua praesentia.

(This rule is the trochaic counterpart of the 'law of the split anapaest' in iambic verse, **38B**; and it accounts for the comparative rarity of the dactyl in the *fourth* foot of the septenarius, which is nearly always followed by word-division, **48B**.)

The rules stated in this section—which may well appear complicated—will be grasped far more readily after consideration of **30B**, a paragraph which deals in detail with the essential unity of iambic and trochaic verse.]

A

50A. The full scheme of the trochaic tetrameter is thus as follows:

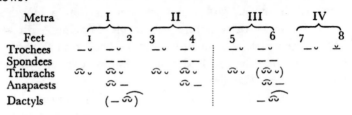

Metra	I			II		III		IV	
Feet	1	2	3	4	5	6	7	8
Trochees	— ᵕ	— ᵕ	— ᵕ	— ᵕ	— ᵕ	— ᵕ	— ᵕ	— ᵕ
Spondees		— —		— —		— —		
Tribrachs	ᵕᵕ ᵕ	ᵕᵕ ᵕ	ᵕᵕ ᵕ	ᵕᵕ ᵕ	ᵕᵕ ᵕ	(ᵕᵕ ᵕ)		
Anapaests		ᵕᵕ —		ᵕᵕ —		ᵕᵕ —		
Dactyls		(— ᵕᵕ)				— ᵕᵕ		

Other trochaic lengths

[**51A.** *Trochaic scazon.* A 'limping' tetrameter or 'scazon' (cf. **42A**) with dragged penultimate syllable, is found in the fragments of Varro: e.g. *fr.* 21B

      antesignani quadratis multisignibus tecti

      — ᵕ — —   — ᵕ — —   — ᵕ — ᵕ   — — —]

[**52A.** *Trochaic dimeter.* The trochaic dimeter — ᵕ — ᵛ — ᵕ — ᵛ plays no independent part in 'type A' verse (cf. opposite page for its 'type B' counterpart): but for Boethius' startling fusion of this length with *ionic* elements, cf. **126.**]

↓
B

50B. The full scheme of the trochaic septenarius is thus as follows:

Metra	I		II		III		IV	
Feet	1	2	3	4	5	6	7	8
Trochees and spondees	— ⌣	— ⌣	— ⌣	— ⌣	— ⌣	— ⌣	— ⌣ —	
Tribrachs and anapaests	⌣⌣ ⌣	⌣⌣ ⌣	⌣⌣ ⌣	⌣⌣ ⌣	⌣⌣ ⌣	⌣⌣ ⌣	⌣⌣ ⌣	
Dactyls	— ⌣⌣	— ⌣⌣	— ⌣⌣	(— ⌣⌣)	— ⌣⌣	— ⌣⌣		

Other trochaic lengths

52B. *Trochaic quaternarius.* This line (which has no 'type A' counterpart in common use) is basically a line of four trochaic feet, which makes occasional appearances in Roman comedy. Its scheme is effectually that of the first four feet of the septenarius described above, spondaic and resolved feet being admitted in the same fashion (cf. **47B**):

$$\overset{\smile\smile}{\underset{\smile\smile}{}}\ \overset{\smile}{\underset{\smile\smile}{}} \quad \overset{\smile\smile}{\underset{\smile\smile}{}}\ \overset{\smile}{\underset{\smile\smile}{}} \quad \overset{\smile\smile}{\underset{\smile\smile}{}}\ \overset{\smile}{\underset{\smile\smile}{}} \quad \overset{\smile\smile}{\underset{}{}}\ \overset{\smile}{\underset{}{}}$$

But resolution is commoner in the early part of the line, as in the following short 'system' of quaternarii (Pl. *Bacch.* 968-74)

cepi spolia, is nunc ducentos	— —	⌣⌣ —	— ⌣	— —
nummos Philǐppos militi, quos	— —	⌣⌣ —	— ⌣	— —
dare se promisit, dabit, nunc	⌣⌣ —	— —	— ⌣	— —
alteris etiam ducentis	— ⌣	— ⌣⌣	— ⌣	— —
usus est, qui dispensentur	— ⌣	— —	— —	— —
Ilio capto, ut sit mulsum	— ⌣	— —	— —	— —
qui triumphent milites.	— ⌣	— —	— ⌣	—

(For the 'catalexis' of the final line, cf. **54B**.) The quaternarius is not common in itself, but is an important element in the structure of the octonarius: cf. next section.

A

↓
B

53B. *Trochaic octonarius.* This line has no counterpart common in 'type A' verse, and its Greek equivalent is hardly found in surviving literature. It makes occasional appearances in Roman comedy, usually to denote great excitement. Basically it is the equivalent of two quaternarii as described above, or of eight complete trochaic feet; as in other trochaic lengths of this type, the trochee — ⌣ is freely replaced by the spondee — —, tribrach ⌢⌣ and anapaest ⌢ — ; the dactyl — ⌢ is admitted to all feet except the fourth and eighth[1].

e.g. Ter. *H.T.* 567–9

hominem amicum recipere ad te atque eius amicam subigitare

vel heri in vino quam inmodestus fuïsti, — factum, — quam
    molestus.

ut equidem, ita me dï } ament, metui, quid futurum denique
    esset!

⌢⌣   — —   ⌢⌣   — —   ⌢⌣ — —   ⌢⌣ — —

⌢ —   — —   — ⌣   — —   — — — —   — ⌣ — —

⌢⌣   ⌢ —   ⌢ —   ⌢ —   — ⌣ — —   — ⌣ — —

[Sometimes (as at *H.T.* 572ff.) the octonarius is found alternating with the septenarius (**47B**), which of course differs from it in length by only one element:

    esto, at certe ut hinc concedas aliquo ab ore eorum
        aliquantisper.

    multa fert lubido: ea facere prohibet tua praesentia.

    — —   — ⌣   — — — —   ⌢⌣ — —   ⌢ — — —

    — ⌣   — ⌣   — ⌢⌢ ⌣   ⌢ — ⌢ —   — ⌣ —]

[There is always word-division (diaeresis, **18**) after the fourth foot of the octonarius: the effect of this is that often the line reads like two separate quaternarii (**52B**), and this effect is sometimes enhanced by hiatus (**15**) at the diaeresis, as at Pl. *Bacch.* 612

    petulans, protervo, iracundo} | animo, indomito, incogitato
    ⌢ —   — —   — — — — | ⌢ —   ⌢ —   — ⌣ — —

[1 *Word-division.* The same rules apply as in the septenarius—cf. **49B**.]

A

54A. *Trochaic dimeter catalectic.* This line [sometimes known as *lecythion*] is basically a trochaic dimeter with the final syllable suppressed

e.g.   pauperem laboribus

                 $-\smile-\smile \quad -\smile-$ (H. *Od.* ii.18.39)

and is in fact the equivalent of the second half of the tetrameter described above,

e.g.   . . . quique amavit cras amet   in ex. **47A**a.

    Horace makes use of the line in one ode (ii.18), alternating it with a catalectic iambic trimeter (cf. **44A**b), e.g. 1–2

     non ebur neque aureum $-\smile-\smile \quad -\smile-$

     mea renidet in domo lacunar. $\overset{\smile}{-}-\smile- \quad \overset{\smile}{-}-\smile- \quad \smile--$

55A. *Ithyphallic.* This name is given to the length $-\smile-\smile--$ (one syllable shorter than the preceding example), e.g. *veris et Favoni.*

    The ithyphallic is common in Greek lyric, but in 'type A' Latin verse (cf. opposite page for 'type B') it is only found as a constituent part of a line sometimes called 'archilochean', in which it follows four dactylic feet: e.g. H. *Od.* i.4.9

     nunc decet aut viridi nitidum caput impedire myrto

     $-\smile\smile \quad -\smile\smile \quad -\smile\smile \quad -\smile\smile \mid -\smile-\smile--$

Horace uses this compound in alternation with the same catalectic iambic trimeter (cf. **44A**) which appeared in the last section (**54A**): e.g. *Od.* i.4.1–2

       solvitur acris hiems grata vice veris et Favoni,

       trahuntque siccas machinae carinas.

B

For similar hiatus at the midpoint of the longer iambic and anapaestic lines, cf. **43B**, **44B**, **106–7**.]

The scheme of the octonarius is thus

‿‿ ⏓ ‿‿ ⏓ ‿‿ ⏓ ‿‿ ⏑ ⦙ ‿‿ ⏓ ‿‿ ⏓ ‿‿ ⏓ ‿‿ —

[**54B.** *Trochaic quaternarius catalectic*. The term catalexis is employed when a line is docked of its final syllable, as at the end of the trochaic 'system' quoted above (**52B**)

    qui triumphent milites.   — ⏑ — —   — ⏑ —   (Pl. *Bacch.* 974)

This line (which is actually the equivalent of the second half of the septenarius) is occasionally found among octonarii (**53B**) and the like (e.g. Ter. *H.T.* 178) or used in its own right, as at Pl. *Epid.* 3ff.

    —respice vero, Thesprio. —oh!   — ⏕ — —   — ⏑ —
       Epidicumne ego conspicor?   ⏕ ⏑ — ⏕   — ⏑ —
    —sati' recte oculis uteris.   ⏕ — ⏕ —   — ⏑ —
    —salve. —di dent quae velis.   — — — —   — ⏑ —

Cf. the stricter 'type A' counterpart on the facing page.]

[**55B.** *Ithyphallic, etc*. The name ithyphallic is given to the trochaic length — ⏑ — ⏑ — —, whose 'type A' form is described on the facing page. This line seldom appears in Roman comedy, e.g. Pl. *Cas.* 830

       rem accipe hanc a nobis   — ⏑ — —   — —

Together with a still shorter trochaic length — ⏑ — ⏑ — it is sometimes found in cretic verse: for this cf. **118**.]

A

[cf. further **96**; and for the ithyphallic's *apparent* part in saturnian verse, cf. **24**.]

Iambic and trochaic lengths among other metres

56A. It was a common practice of the Greek lyric poets to mingle various metres within the same stanza; this practice is less favoured in Latin verse, where metrical structures are at any rate simpler (cf. **6**) and there is some tendency towards a more rigid categorisation.

In the case of iambic/trochaic verse, however, a special link with dactylic elements is to be seen in a few of the *Odes* and *Epodes* of Horace, [imitated in this respect by later poets such as Ausonius and Boethius]. For such mixtures—largely drawn from the Greek poet Archilochus—cf. **93–96**.

B

Iambic and trochaic lengths among other metres

56B. As stated on the opposite page (**56A**), it is not on the whole a common practice of the *Roman* poets to mingle different metres within the same stanza, or passage. Some exceptions are provided in the *cantica* of Plautus, where isolated iambic or trochaic lengths occasionally appear among other metres—notably in cretic or bacchiac surroundings: for this cf. **114**, **119**.

In addition, it is common enough in Roman comedy for iambic and trochaic lines to alternate with one another. This fact is not surprising when it is borne in mind how similar the two movements in fact are (cf. **29**, **30B**), but it can make actual recognition difficult, especially in the case of the longer dialogue lines (octonarii and septenarii—**43B**, **44B**, **47B**, **53B**) which mingle particularly freely—e.g. at Pl. *Pseud.* 225–9

> tu autem, quae pro capite argentum mihi iam iamque
>   semper numeras,
> ea pacisci modo scis, sed quod pacta's non scis solvere,
> Phoenicium, tibi ego haec loquor, deliciae summatum
>   virum;
> nisi hodie mi ex fundis tuōrum amicorum omne huc penus
>   adfertur,
> cras, Phoenicium, phoeniceo corio invises pergulam.

— —	— — |	⌢ —	— — |	⌢ —	— ◡	| — — ⌢ — troch. oct.
⌢ ◡	— — |	⌢ —	— — |	— —	— —	| — ◡ — troch. sept.
— — ◡	— |⌢	— ◡	— |	— ⌢ —	— |—	— ◡ — iamb. oct.
⌢ ◡	— — |	— —	— ◡ |	— —	— —	| ⌢ — — — troch. oct.
— —	— ◡ |	— —	⌢ — |	⌢ —	— —	| — ◡ — troch. sept.

CHAPTER 5

Dactylic Verse and Simple Dactylic Compounds

Basic dactylic rhythm and metron

57. As seen in the last chapter, the iambic and trochaic movements run very similarly, owing (primarily) to the similarity of the actual feet involved, ⏑ – and – ⏑. There is an equally obvious similarity between the anapaest ⏑⏑ – and the dactyl – ⏑⏑; but in this case the two rhythms run into rather different types of verse. Consequently the anapaestic rhythm is treated in a separate chapter (Ch. 6) from the dactylic.

58. The basic dactylic metron, or unit of movement, is the single foot – ⏑⏑. The only substitute for the dactyl admitted is the spondee – –; the scheme of the metron is thus – ⏖. (The *last* metron of a line or period tends to take the spondaic form (e.g. in the hexameter), and in this case the final syllable is *anceps* (**19**)

. . . – ⏖ – ⏖ – ⏓)

59. *Catalexis.* The term 'catalexis' is employed when a line is docked of its final element—in the case of a 'catalectic' dactylic line, the effect is that the final double-short of a dactyl (or the final long syllable of a spondee) is suppressed:

. . . – ⏖ – ⏖ –

DACTYLIC HEXAMETER

60. This familiar line is the vehicle for heroic epic, for didactic, satirical, pastoral and much other poetry, and plays its part in such combinations as the elegiac couplet (**78**ff.) and certain lyric structures (cf. **91**, **92**, **94**).

Dactylic Verse and Simple Dactylic Compounds

In terms of the metrical elements involved, the line remained basically unchanged from its earliest Greek usage, consisting of six metra of the simple type outlined above (58), of which the fifth was *usually* an uncontracted dactyl and the sixth *always* a spondee [or, with final *anceps* (19), a trochee — ᷜ]:

$$- \underline{\smallsmile\smallsmile} \quad - \underline{\smallsmile\smallsmile} \quad - \underline{\smallsmile\smallsmile} \quad - \underline{\smallsmile\smallsmile} \quad - (\underline{\smallsmile\smallsmile}) \quad - \underline{\smile}$$

e.g. ἄνδρα μοι ἔννεπε, Μοῦσα, πολύτροπον, ὃς μάλα πολλὰ
πλάγχθη, ἐπεὶ Τροίης ἱερὸν πτολίεθρον ἔπερσε.

(Homer, *Odyssey* i.1–2)

Owing to the richness of the Latin language in quantitatively long syllables, spondaic feet are distinctly commoner in Latin than in Greek hexameters: this may be seen from a comparison of the above example with the opening lines of Virgil's epic:

> arma virumque cano, Troiae qui primus ab oris
> Italiam fato profugus Lavinaque venit
> litora—multum ille et terris iactatus et alto
> vi superum, saevae memorem Iunonis ab iram.

$$- \smallsmile\smallsmile \quad - \smallsmile\smallsmile \quad - - \quad - - \quad - \smallsmile\smallsmile - -$$
$$- \smallsmile\smallsmile \quad - - \quad - \smallsmile\smallsmile \quad - - \quad - \smallsmile\smallsmile - -$$
$$- \smallsmile\smallsmile \quad - - \quad - - \quad - - \quad - \smallsmile\smallsmile - -$$
$$- \smallsmile\smallsmile \quad - - \quad - \smallsmile\smallsmile \quad - - \quad - \smallsmile\smallsmile - - \quad \text{(V. } Aen.\text{i.1–4)}$$

Markedly spondaic or dactylic lines are not uncommon in the work of Ennius (the first Roman adaptor of the hexameter); later writers aimed on the whole at a more careful balance between the two types of metron. From early times there is a tendency towards a dactylic *opening* to the line (as in all four lines of the last example). The exceptional charm of Virgil's hexameter (never matched even by his most strenuous imitators) lies largely in his use of sense-pauses at different stages of the line (for which cf. 77), in his judicious interplay of dactyls and spondees, and in his cumulative use of one foot or the other for special effect, e.g.

quadrupedante putrem sonitu quatit ungula campum

(*Aen.* viii.596)

illi inter sese multa vi bracchia tollunt.   (*Aen.* viii.452)

or of elision (15) which is noticeably commoner in his works than in other hexameter writers (though used sparingly near the end of the line), and which again can produce a striking effect, as in

monstr(um) horrend(um) inform(e) ingens, cui lumen
ademptum   (*Aen.* iii.658)

[Spondaic feet are noticeably more frequent in the 'conversational' hexameters of Horace's *Satires*; dactyls on the whole are commoner when the hexameter is used as a component in lyric structures or in the elegiac couplet, but even in his pure hexameter poetry Ovid uses a high proportion of dactyls.]

61. The following additional points should be observed:

[(a) Ennius gives two or three apparent instances of resolution in the opening element of the line—producing an anapaest or 'proceleusmatic' in the first foot, e.g.

mĕlănūrum turdum merulamque umbramque marinam.
                                         (*Varia* 42V)
căpĭtĭbŭ' nutantis pinos rectosque cupressos   (*Ann.* 490)]

(b) A spondaic fifth foot is perceptibly rarer even than in Greek hexameters. Together with certain other 'Alexandrian' ornaments, it is a special affectation of the neoteric Catullus, who at one point (64.78–80) gives three successive instances, e.g. 78

electos iuvenes simul et decus īnnūptārūm.

The fourth foot of such lines is nearly always a dactyl, as in the above example.

This type of line (known as *spondeiazon*) is used occasionally by Virgil, progressively more rarely by his successors. In Virgil's usage an intentionally heavy effect can often be traced, e.g.

proximus huic, longo sed proximus īntērvāllō   (*Aen.* v.320)

and the 'Greek' effect of such lines is sometimes heightened by other irregularities such as hiatus (**15**), as in

stant et iuniperi } et castaneae } hīrsūtāē   (*Ecl.* 7.53)

cf. further **74.**

(c) As stated above, the final syllable of the line is *anceps*—i.e. there is not *synaphea* (**19**) between lines. An exception is provided by occasional 'hypermetric' elision (**15**), e.g.

quo super atra silex iam iam lapsura cadentiqu(e)

imminet adsimilis.   (V. *Aen.* vi.602–3)

This practice is almost confined to Virgil (some twenty cases): there are very few instances in earlier or later writers[1]. Usually the sense runs closely on into the following line; in most cases the elided syllable is -*que* (often a repeated -*que*), and sometimes a special effect can be seen, as in the above example, or in

aut dulcis musti Volcano decoquit umor(em)

et foliis undam trepidi despumat aeni.   (V. *Georg.* i. 295–6)

(d) Unfinished lines or 'half-lines' (actually ranging from one to four feet in length) occur about 60 times in Virgil's *Aeneid*, and nowhere else—a clear indication that their cause is incompletion, and not intentional variation.

Development of the hexameter: rules for word-division

62. In the development of the Latin hexameter, much the most noticeable feature is the growing regard for principles of word-division, especially in the centre and at the end of the line. These will shortly be analysed in some detail (**64**ff.); here they may be broadly summarised as follows:

(a) *Central caesura.* Most Greek hexameters have word-division (caesura, **18**) *either* after the first syllable of the third foot, as in

πλάγχθη, ἐπεὶ Τροίης ┆ ἱερὸν πτολίεθρον ἔπερσε

or after the second syllable of a third foot dactyl, as in

ἄνδρα μοι ἔννεπε, Μοῦσα, ┆ πολύτροπον, ὃς μάλα πολλά

In Latin, the same principle can be seen as early as Ennius, whose exceptions (though notorious and uncouth) are genuinely rare; and later hexameter writers became progressively stricter in this principle. The prevailing type of caesura is the first (the

[1 Lucretius has 1 example; Catullus 2 (1 in elegiacs); Ovid 3; Valerius Flaccus 1. Ennius may also have used the device.]

'strong' or 'masculine' caesura); the second type ('weak' or 'feminine') is notably rarer in Latin than in Greek, and in developed hexameter writings is nearly always subordinated to more vital 'strong' caesuras in adjoining feet. In general, the Roman poets show an increasing tendency towards word-division within (rather than between) the central feet of the line—not only the third foot.

(b) *Line ending*. While the Greek hexameter writers observed no strict rules for the ending of the line, a *tendency* towards a disyllabic or trisyllabic final word is observable even in Ennius, and the tendency becomes a *rule* in the hexameters of Cicero, Catullus and the Augustan and silver age writers, although it is observed less strictly by the satiric poets (especially Horace).

[63. In the establishment of these principles for caesura and line-ending, it is probable that considerations of word-accent played a significant rôle (cf. Ch. 3, esp. 27). The effect (which is possibly also the cause) of such rules is that word-accent tends to coincide with the beginning of the foot in the fifth and sixth places (as though to emphasise the 'pulse' of the rhythm), and to conflict in the centre of the line; and this tendency increases with the 'strictness' of the writer in these respects, as will be seen in the following paragraphs.]

64. In the observance of these principles for word-division, three broad classes of Latin hexameter writing can be distinguished:

(1) *Early usage*. From Ennius to Lucretius. During this period the tendencies already observable in Ennius are gradually strengthened; the hexameters of Lucretius stand about midway between those of Ennius and the fully developed 'Augustan' type.

(2) *Fully developed type*. Cicero and Catullus, Virgil, Ovid and post-Augustan writers of epic and other serious poetry (e.g. Lucan, Statius, Valerius Flaccus and Silius Italicus; and still later poets such as Ausonius and Claudian). This type also includes the hexameters found in elegiac and lyric poetry.

[It may seem strange that Catullus should represent so marked an advance on his contemporary Lucretius, but the following facts help to explain this: (a) the more unmanageable vocabulary of Lucretius' technical terms; (b) Catullus' strong interest (already mentioned, 1) in poetic sophistication; (c) the influence of Cicero's rigidly careful hexameter writing.

The 'classical' principles for central caesura and line-ending, already established in the hexameters of Cicero and Catullus, vary little after their day, either in the Augustan age or in silver Latin practice. Virgil imposed one or two extra refinements (cf. esp. **69**), but his positive advance lies not so much in the observance of such restrictions as in his rare but effective breach of them, and in his equally effective use of word-division and pauses at other points of the line—cf. **77.**]

(3) *Conversational type.* The looser writing of the satiric poets (especially Horace: Juvenal's hexameters are more polished). (These writers adhere in general to the principles of class (2), but breaches are more common—especially at the end of the line.)

A. Centre of Line

65. Ennius gives a few examples of lines without a central caesura, e.g. the famous

> sparsis hastis longis campus splendet et horret

(Enn. Varia 14V)

and   poste recumbite, vestraque pectora pellite tonsis

(Ann. 230)

But these are exceptional instances. Even in Ennius there is an overwhelming tendency for words to end within, rather than after, the central feet of the line; in fact only about 4 per cent of his hexameters lack a central caesura of the 'classical' type, and this percentage decreases rapidly in the work of his successors.

66. *Main central caesura.* As stated above (**62**a), the dominant central caesura in the Latin hexameter is the 'strong' caesura after the first syllable of the third foot, as in

(a) arma virumque cano ⋮ Troiae qui primus ab oris

(V. Aen. i.1)

Alternatively, an elision before the third foot seems to have been regarded as equivalent to a strong caesura within it, e.g.

(b) et genus invisum ⁞ et rapti Ganymedis honores.

(*Aen.* i.28)

[But such elision is usually combined with strong caesuras in both the second and fourth feet,

e.g. (c) contendunt ⁞ petere ⁞ et Libyae ⁞ vertuntur ad oras.

(*Aen.* i.158)

and this effect should be compared with (f) below.]

The 'weak' third foot caesura is far less common in Latin than in Greek (and is noticeably rarer still in the hexameters of elegiac poetry): in the most developed type of hexameter verse (cf. 64) it is nearly always combined with 'strong' caesura in the fourth foot *at least*, e.g.

(d) armaque Amyclaeumque ⁞ canem ⁞ Cressamque
    pharetram (*V. Georg.* iii.345)

and usually *also* with 'strong' caesura in the second foot, e.g.

(e) insequitur ⁞ clamorque ⁞ virum ⁞ stridorque rudentum.

(*Aen.* i.87)

In such cases, indeed, the 'weak' third foot caesura seems less vital than the two 'strong' breaks in the second and fourth feet, which occasionally suffice by themselves without *any* word-division within the third foot: e.g.

(f) iamque vale: ⁞ feror ingenti ⁞ circumdata nocte.

(*V. Georg.* iv.497)

67. It should be noted in addition that—in the developed hexameter form (cf. 64)—word-division very rarely occurs at the end of the second foot unless there is also caesura within that foot[1]. Thus lines such as the following are 'correct' since *both* divisions occur:

(a) quam tu urbem, ⁞ soror, ⁞ hanc ⁞ cernes, quae surgere
    regna. (*Aen.* iv.41)

    Anna soror, ⁞ quae ⁞ me ⁞ suspensam insomnia terrent

(*Aen.* iv.9)

[1 This 'rule' is imposed by considerations of word-accent, for which cf. 69.]

credo equidem, ǀ nec ǀ vana ǀ fides, genus esse deorum

(*Aen.* iv.12)

(and cf. also **66f** above); examples such as the following are rare in the strictest verse, and derive a possibly intended effect from their rarity:

(b) et cum frigida ǀ mors ǀ anima seduxerit artus

(*Aen.* iv.385)

armentarius ǀ Afer ǀ agit tectumque laremque

(*Georg.* iii.344)

But this particular refinement is not observed in earlier hexameter writers (**64**), and Lucretius in particular gives many examples which would be irregular in Virgilian verse, e.g.

(c) ergo vivida ǀ vis ǀ animi pervicit, et extra . . .

(Lucr. i.72)

religionibus ǀ atque ǀ minis obsistere vatum

(Lucr. i.109)

cui simul infula ǀ virgineos circumdata comptus

(Lucr. i.87)

And the 'rule' is occasionally broken by Horace in his satiric hexameters, e.g.

ille Tigellius ǀ hoc. ǀ Caesar qui cogere posset

(H. *Sat.* i.3.4)

68. It was observed above (**66**) that the 'weak' third foot caesura is regularly followed, in the 'developed' type (cf. **64**), by a 'strong' caesura in the fourth foot. As in the case of the last restriction (cf. **67b**), exceptions to this rule are rare, and often derive effect from their context, e.g.

(a) praecipitat ǀ suadentque ǀ cadentia sidera somnos.

(V. *Aen.* ii.9)

spargens umida mella ǀ soporiferumque papaver

(*Aen.* iv.486)

mersatur ǀ missusque ǀ secundo defluit amni

(*Georg.* iii.447)

(The last type is particularly rare, probably because of the false illusion of line-ending produced by *secundo*.)

Again, earlier writers do not observe this refinement: e.g.
(b) quid nequeat, ┊ finita ┊ potestas denique cuique
(Lucr. i.76)
and it is sometimes disregarded in satiric verse, as in
qui moechis ┊ non vultis ┊, ut omni parte laborent
(H. Sat. i.2.38)
[The Roman poets[1] do *not* follow the Greeks' strenuous avoidance of weak caesura in the fourth foot; but such caesura is used sparingly nevertheless, perhaps because of the 'false cadence' produced by effects such as
saxa sonant, vocisque offensa ┊ resultat ┊ imago.
(V. Georg. iv.50)]

[**69.** *Word-accent.* As stated in an earlier paragraph (**63**), the influence of word-accent (cf. Ch. 3) has often been thought to play a vital part in determining the caesura principles just observed. It will be seen from the reiteration of some previous examples that conflict between the beginning of the foot and accent *predominates* in the centre of 'orthodox' types of line:

árma vir|úmque cán|o Troí|ae quí [primus ab oris
inséqui|tur clam|órque vír|um stri [dorque rudentum
iámque vál|e: féror| ingén|ti cir[cumdata nocte
crédo équid|em néc|vána fíd|es génus [esse deorum.
quám tu úr|bem, sóror, | hánc cér|nes, quaé [surgere regna.
while the Lucretian types largely abandoned by Virgil (cf. **67b–c, 68**) fail to secure this conflict to the same extent:
érgo | vívida | vís ánim|i per [vicit et extra
rèligi|ónibus | átque mín|is ob[sistere vatum.
praecípit|at suad|éntque cad|éntia [sidera somnos.
mereá | tur mis|súsque sec|úndo [defluit amni.
It will be seen later (**75**) that, conversely, accent normally *coincides* with the beginning of the fifth and sixth feet (this is in fact the case in all the above examples).

The position of the fourth foot in this respect is interesting. Not only Lucretius, but also the more sophisticated poets Cicero and Catullus (cf. **64**), have a strong tendency towards

[[1] Except Catullus, in poem 64 *only*.]

accentual coincidence in this foot, particularly when it is a spondee, as

Peliaco quondam prog|nátac | vertice pinus   (Cat. 64.1)

(Such coincidence occurs in 12 of the first 15 lines of Cat. 64.) One of Virgil's most notable advances lies in his restriction of this rhythm: it is by no means *rare* in his work, e.g.

tantae molis erat Ro|mánam | condere gentem   (V. *Aen.* i.33)

but is very distinctly less common than in previous poets. Thus in *Aen.* i.1 he writes

. . . Troí|ae quí | primus ab oris

where earlier poets might have been content with

. . . quí | Tróiae | primus ab oris.]

B. End of the Line

(1) *Early usage*

70. *Ennius.* Greek hexameter writers placed few restrictions on word-division at the end of the line; but from the start their Latin successors showed a strong preference for a final word of two or three syllables, and this ending (as will be seen in **72**) became the fixed rule in the fully developed hexameter form. Even in Ennius, about 80 per cent of hexameter endings show the two 'classical' types of ending, e.g.

undique conveniunt velut imber tela *tribuno*:
configunt parmam, tinnit hastilibus *umbo*.   (*Ann.* 401-2)

But endings of four or five syllables are common enough, as in

'nec mi aurum posco nec mi pretium *dederitis*:
non cauponantes bellum sed *belligerantes*'   (*Ann.* 194-5)

There are a few examples of still longer endings, and (much more than any subsequent poet except for the satirists) he affects the monosyllabic close, as in the famous

unus homo nobis cunctando restituit *rem*.   (*Ann.* 370)

71. *Lucretius.* At first sight, Lucretian endings seem scarcely more strict than those of Ennius: about one-eighth of Lucretius' hexameters end 'irregularly' by the Augustan canon, e.g.

quae mare navigerum, quae terras *frugiferentis*

concelebras, per te quoniam genus omne *animantum*

(Lucr. i.3–4)

significant imitum perculsae corda tua *vi*.   (Lucr. i.13)

But one Lucretian advance is striking, and foreshadows later rules: although endings of four or five syllables are common enough, a final four-syllable word (or word-group) is in most cases preceded by a monosyllable. Thus endings such as the following are common

(a) . . . nec minitanti

. . . dum satis acris

the following type is notably rarer

(b) . . . species ratioque.

. . . sed eo magis acrem.

[Type (a) ensures coincidence of word-accent with the openings of the last two feet—cf. **75.**]

(2) *Developed type*

72. In the fully developed hexameters of Cicero, Catullus and later poets (cf. **64**), the tendencies already noted have hardened into rules. Nearly all lines end with a three-syllable word or word-group, as in

(a) silvestrem tenui Musam meditaris *avena*   (V. *Ecl.* 1.2)

or with a two-syllable word, as in

(b) Tityre, tu patulae recubans sub tegmine *fagi*   (Ecl. 1.1)

An ending of *two* disyllables is avoided unless they are preceded by a monosyllable, as in

(c) bina die siccant ovis ubera: *quos tibi servo*   (*Ecl.* 2.42)

[This last restriction is foreshadowed by Lucretius: cf. **71.**]

73. Exceptions to the above 'rules' are very rare in Virgil and his successors, and consequently are the more effective on their occasional appearances:

(a) solus ego in Pallanta feror, *soli mihi Pallas*

(V. *Aen.* x.442)(cf. **72c**)

(b) dant sonitu ingentem perfractaque *quadrupedantum*
(*Aen.* xi.614)

(c) sternitur exanimisque tremens procumbit humi *bos*
(*Aen.* v.481)

(d) Martius ille aeris rauci canor increpat, *et vox* . . .
(*Georg.* iv.71)

[An ending of *two* monosyllables—as in (d)—is much less rare than that of a single monosyllable, such as (c): cf. **75b**.]

74. *Greek imitations.* Abnormal line-endings are particularly associated with Greek derivatives, or with lines containing an idea of eastern effeminacy, e.g.

(a) et nunc ille Paris cum semiviro *comitatu* (V. *Aen.* iv.215)
In such cases, the line often shows other abnormalities—e.g. an irregular central caesura, as in

(b) per conubia nostra, per inceptos *hymenaeos* (Aen. iv.316)
or hiatus (**15**), as in

(c) aetas Lucinam iustosque pati } *hymenaeos*   (*Georg.* iii.60)

(d) lamentis gemituque et femineo } *ululatu*   (*Aen.* iv.667)
and (with a spondaic fifth foot, cf. **61b**)

(e) Ardea Crustumerique et turrigerae } *Antemnae.*
(*Aen.* vii.631)
[For such 'Grecisms' in general, cf. further **15**.]

[**75.** *Word-accent.* It has already been observed (**63**) that word-accent is often thought to play a vital part in these principles for line-ending. A reiteration of some previous examples will show that in the 'orthodox' endings the closing feet of the line begin with accented syllables, while unorthodox endings produce some conflict at least:

(a) *orthodox*   medi]t áris av|éna
primus ab | óris
tégmine | fági
quós tíbi | sérvo

Dactylic Verse and Simple Dactylic Compounds

(b) *unorthodox*   só]li míhi | Pállas
qu⟨à⟩drupe | dántum
pro] cúmbit hú|mi bós
íncrepat | ét vóx
incép]t os hyme|naéos[1]

These examples may be compared with those showing the pre-dominating *conflict* between foot and accent in the centre of the line—cf. 69.]

(3) *Conversational type*

76. The satiric poets observe, in the main, the above principles for line-ending; but breaches are somewhat more common than in more serious verse. Endings of four or five syllables occur here and there, e.g.

cum populum gregibus comitum premit hic *spoliator*

(Juv. 1.46)

quandoquidem inter nos sanctissima *divitiarum*   (Juv. 1.112)

But most notable is the frequency of monosyllabic endings, e.g.

. . . pensilibus plumis atque illinc despiciat *nos* (Juv. 1.159)

'nil satis est' inquit, 'quia tanti quantum habeas *sis*.'

(H. *Sat.* i.1.62)

And it is particularly typical of this type of verse for a mono-syllable at the end of a line to be connected closely with the following line as in

cantat, et apponit 'meus est amor huic similis; *nam*
transvolat in medio posita et fugientia captat.'

(H. *Sat.* i.1.107–8)

General flow of hexameter verse

77. A great part of the charm of developed hexameter verse lies in its easy flow from line to line, and in the judicious use of pauses within lines. Favourite places for such pauses are the middle of the second, third and fourth feet; effective also is a pause at the end of the first foot (usually a dactylic word in an

[1 It should be noticed that the type *néc mini|tánti* does produce coincidence. It was seen in **71** that Lucretius prefers this type to the conflicting *incép|tos hyme|naéos*, and it has never been satisfactorily explained why Virgil eschews both types equally.]

emphatic position) or after a dactylic fourth foot (the 'bucolic pause', particularly common in the Greek pastoral poets).

Virgil and Ovid (in the hexameters of the *Metamorphoses*) are masters of such rhythmical skill. The subject is too large to be treated at length in this book; for the descriptive power which the hexameter can gain from this skill the reader is referred especially to the concluding part of Virgil's *First Georgic*, from which the following is a striking extract:

> saepe etiam immensum caelo venit agmen aquarum
> et foedam glomerant tempestatem imbribus atris
> collectae ex alto nubes; ruit arduus aether,
> et pluvia ingenti sata laeta boumque labores
> diluit; implentur fossae et cava flumina crescunt
> cum sonitu fervetque fretis spirantibus aequor.
> ipse pater media nimborum in nocte corusca
> fulmina molitur dextra: quo maxima motu
> terra tremit; fugere ferae et mortalia corda
> per gentis humilis stravit pavor: ille flagranti
> aut Athon aut Rhodopen aut alta Ceraunia telo
> deicit; ingeminant Austri et densissimus imber;
> nunc nemora ingenti vento, nunc litora plangunt.
>
> (V. *Georg.* i.322–34)

THE ELEGIAC COUPLET

78. *Dactylic 'pentameter'.* It was seen in **66** that *most* dactylic hexameters have a 'strong' caesura (or word-division) after the first syllable of the third foot. The name 'hemiepes' [i.e. 'half an epic verse'] is sometimes applied to the segment preceding such a caesura—the equivalent of $2\frac{1}{2}$ dactylic feet, e.g.

arma virumque cano. — ⏑⏑ — ⏑⏑ —

When this segment is repeated a line is produced which is loosely called the 'pentameter': but spondees are rigorously excluded from the second segment of the line, so that its scheme is

— ⏑⏑ — ⏑⏑ —   — ⏑⏑ — ⏑⏑ —

e.g.   arbor habet frondes, pabula semper humus.

(Ov. *Fasti* v.208)

This line is exceedingly common as the second part of the elegiac couplet, which is next to be described; elsewhere it hardly occurs (but cf. 92c).

79. The elegiac couplet consists of an alternation of dactylic hexameter (60ff.) with the 'pentameter' just described:

$$- \cup\cup \quad - \cup\cup \quad - \cup\cup \quad - \cup\cup \quad - \cup\cup \quad - -$$

$$- \cup\cup \quad - \cup\cup - \quad - \cup\cup \quad - \cup\cup \quad -$$

It is frequently found in Greek poetry, e.g.

Ἀστὴρ πρὶν μὲν ἔλαμπες ἐνὶ ζωοῖσιν Ἑῷος·
νῦν δὲ θανὼν λάμπεις Ἕσπερος ἐν φθιμένοις.

(Plato *fr.* 5D²)

This couplet occasionally occurs in the remains of early Latin literature, but does not reach much literary importance before the time of Catullus. Elegiac verse was in fact moulded and formalised to Roman taste rather later than pure hexameter verse: this is well demonstrated by Catullus, whose hexameters (as observed above, 64) already conform to Augustan restrictions, while his pentameters are as uncouth as those to be found in Ennius' epitaphs[1]. However, in the Augustan age Tibullus, Propertius and Ovid progressively imposed on the pentameter a strictness of form exceeding even that of the hexameter.

80. Elegiac couplets are mainly self-contained entities: the sense frequently runs on from hexameter to pentameter, as in

quam bene Saturno vivebant rege, priusquam
tellus in longas est patefacta vias.   (Tib. i.3.35–6)

but the sentence, or at least the clause, normally ends with the couplet, and it is very rare for couplets to be *closely* linked in sense. (Catullus provides some notable exceptions, e.g. 65.10–11.)

Structure of the hexameter in elegiac verse

81. The hexameter of elegiac verse conforms to the same restrictions as in pure hexameter verse of the fully developed type (cf. 64, 72). But a slightly greater strictness of construction can be seen in certain details:

[1] and in intervening epigrammatists such as Q. Lutatius Catulus.]

(a) the central caesura (**66**) is still more rigidly observed: type **66a** predominates, and the only common alternative is **66e**, which is twice as common in Tibullus as in the other Augustan elegists.

(b) rules for line-ending (**72**) are also observed more strictly: exceptional endings are genuinely rare, especially in Ovid, and so are affectations such as hiatus (**15**) and the spondaic fifth foot (**61b**).

(c) especially in Ovid, the texture is light and smooth: this can be seen in the comparative rarity of elision (contrast **60**), and in the increased proportion of dactylic feet, especially at the beginning of the verse.

Structure of the pentameter—general

82. The pentameter is still crude and unformed in the elegiacs of Catullus, as can be seen from the following instance:

quam modo qui me unum atque unicum amicum habuit

(Cat. 73.6)

Its advance to sophistication at the hands of later poets lies chiefly

(a) in the avoidance of heavy elision such as is seen in the above example: the Augustans hardly admit elision at all to the second segment of the line.

(b) in a strengthening tendency for the line to open with a dactylic foot (a tendency also observed in the hexameter, **81c**).

(c) in the growing strictness of the line-ending (cf. **84ff**).

83. *Central caesura.* There is invariably word-division after the first half of the pentameter, as in

Mars ades et nitidas ⋮ casside solve comas.

(Ov. *Fasti* iii.2)

Catullus allows elision over this point, as in the example quoted above (**82**) or in

êi misero eripuist(i) ⋮ omnia nostra bona. (Cat. 77.4)

But such elision is strenuously avoided by later elegiac poets, who furnish hardly any examples (there are two in Propertius). The central caesura may not be preceded by a monosyllable unless there is a break within, as well as after, the second foot, as in

> infelix ⋮ quod ⋮ non ⋮ alter et alter eras.
>
> (Ov. *Fasti* v.226)

This rule is thus broken in

> o di, reddite ⋮ m(i) hoc ⋮ pro pietate mea.
>
> (Cat. 76.26)

[For the same rule at the main caesura of the hexameter cf. **67**: it is probably due to the Roman desire for word-accent to conflict with the opening of the foot at this stage of the line—cf. examples at **69**.]

Structure of pentameter—the line-ending

84. (1) *In Catullus*. The Greek elegiac poets imposed no particular restrictions on the final word of the pentameter. Early examples of Latin elegy show the same freedom; and this freedom is still shared, at first sight, by Catullus, in whose pentameters the final word is regularly of any length from two to five syllables—e.g. (in consecutive pentameters)

> progenies Thiae clara *supervehitur*   (Cat. 66.44)
> per medium classi barbara navit *Athon*   (66.46)
> Iuppiter ut Chalybon omne genus *pereat*   (66.48)
> institit ac ferri stringere *duritiem*   (66.50)

Catullus also gives one example of a monosyllabic ending (*dictaque factaque sunt*, 76.8) and one of seven syllables (*Amphitryoniades*, 68.112).

Nevertheless, even in Catullus' elegies nearly two-fifths of the pentameters are concluded by dissyllabic words (such as *Athon* above); and this proportion, as will be seen, grows startlingly in Augustan elegy.

85. (2) *In Propertius and Tibullus*. The Augustan age coincides with a vast output of elegiac poetry. This reaches its technical perfection in Ovid; but the development of the pentameter from its uncouth Catullan form is chiefly due to Propertius and

106

Tibullus, and probably also to the lost work of the slightly earlier Gallus.

Propertius' early poems show pentameter-endings as variegated as those of Catullus: the first four couplets of his first book end *cupidinibus, pedibus, consilio, deos*. But even at this stage the poet shows a *tendency* towards the last type: 60 per cent of the pentameters of bk. i end disyllabically. And this tendency rapidly becomes a *rule* in Propertius' later work—a rule to which bk. iv yields very few exceptions.

Tibullus, writing at much the same time, likewise shows a strong preference for the disyllabic close, which occurs in more than 90 per cent of his pentameters. He differs from Propertius in a slight preference for the three-syllable ending (e.g. *pedibus*) over the other irregular types; this ending is in general not common in Propertius, and is particularly avoided in his later books, as Ovid was also to avoid it (see below). [Tibullus also markedly avoids placing an iambic word directly before the midpoint of the pentameter—possibly because of the sameness of effect when both halves of the line end similarly, as in Ovid's famous jingle

semibovemque ┆ virum | semivirumque ┆ bovem.

(*Ars Amatoria* ii.24)]

86. (3) *In Ovid.* By the time of Ovid the disyllabic pentameter ending was established, and this poet observed it with depressing rigidity. Very rare concessions are found to four-syllable and five-syllable words, e.g.

et circumfusis invia *fluminibus*   (Ov. *Fasti* v.582)
per non vile tibi nomen *amicitiae*

(Ov. *Epistulae ex Ponto* iv.13.44)

Three-syllable closes are especially avoided, six instances (at the most) occurring in the whole of the poet's vast output. Nearly all the 'irregular' closes are found in Ovid's later poems (*Tristia* and *Ex Ponto*): the *Ars Amatoria* shows no exception to the disyllable rule in 1165 pentameters, and the *Fasti* only two exceptions in nearly 2500 pentameters.

Typical pentameters are thus

> hoc legat et lecto carmine doctus amet.
>
> (Ov. Ars Amatoria i.2)
>
> creditur annosum pertimuisse senem   (*A.A.* i.14)
> granifero solitum cum vehit ore cibum   (*A.A.* i.94)
> flammaque in arguto saepe reperta foro.   (*A.A.* i.80)

[The last two examples show a particular Ovidian tendency to end the two segments of the pentameter with a rhyming epithet and noun.

Ovid also strengthened other restrictions on the final word of the line. This word is nearly always a noun, verb, or pronoun or possessive adjective (e.g. *meus*); ordinary adjectives and adverbs are not admitted unless their sense is emphatic. Finally, although the last syllable of the line is technically *anceps* (**19**), Ovid avoided placing a short final *ă* or *ĕ* in this position.]

87. (4) *In later poets.* The post-Augustan poets followed in the main Ovid's practice in the pentameter; but the disyllabic close, though normal, is not observed by them with quite the same rigidity, and longer endings are not really uncommon.

A particular characteristic of Martial is to break the disyllable 'rule' at the end of an epigram: the irregular word is usually pointed in meaning, and is often a trisyllable, as in

> quod clamas semper, quod agentibus obstrepis, Aeli,
>   non facis hoc gratas: accipis, ut *taceas*.   (Mart. i.95)

[**88.** *Word-accent.* As was seen earlier (**75**), the 'classical' rules for *hexameter* ending ensure that the closing feet of the line begin with accented syllables. In the pentameter the case is different, since the final syllable of the closing sequence ... $-\smile\smile-\smile\smile-$ *cannot* bear an accent unless it is a monosyllabic word. But it *may* be significant that in the 'orthodox' disyllabic ending the previous two feet, at least, open with accented syllables, while the unorthodox type produces some degree of conflict; this will be clear from a repetition of some past examples.

(a) *orthodox* . . . cármine | dóctus á|met.

                         pèrtimu|ísse sé|nem.

                         cúm véhit | óre cí|bum.

                         saépe re|pérta fó|ro.

(b) *unorthodox* . . . ínvia | flumíni|bus.

                         nómen am|icíti|ae.

                         ómne gén|us pére|at.]

General flow of elegiac verse

89. Owing to the self-contained nature of the couplet (cf. **80**), elegiac verse does not offer the scope for periodic writing and graphic pauses that was observed in the hexameter (**77**). Its re-petitive smoothness can appear dull; but when used with skill it is a magnificent vehicle for description and even for story-telling, and the need for rhythmic and verbal balance can be-come an actual advantage. Two short examples will show the different abilities of Propertius and Ovid in this direction:

(a) *descriptive*

> hic erat Arganthi Pege sub vertice montis
> > grata domus Nymphis umida Thyniasin,
> quam supra nullae pendebant debita curae
> > roscida desertis poma sub arboribus;
> et circum irriguo surgebant lilia prato
> > candida purpureis mixta papaveribus.

(Prop. i.20.33-8)

(b) *narrative*

> Silvia Vestalis (quid enim vetat inde moveri?)
> > sacra lavaturas mane petebat aquas.
> ventum erat ad molli declivem tramite ripam:
> > ponitur e summa fictilis urna coma.
> fessa resedit humo ventosque accepit aperto
> > pectore, turbatas restituitque comas.
> dum sedet, umbrosae salices volucresque canorae
> > fecerunt somnos et leve murmur aquae.
> blanda quies furtim victis obrepsit ocellis,
> > et cadit a mento languida facta manus.
> Mars videt hanc visamque cupit potiturque cupita
> > et sua divina furta fefellit ope. (Ov. *Fasti* iii.11–22)

DACTYLS IN LYRIC VERSE

90. In lyric verse (notably that of Horace), various dactylic lines are found shorter than those already described; some of these lengths are occasionally interwoven with other metres, as described below (**92ff**). The spondee is somewhat rarer, especially in short units such as the 'hemiepes' (**78**) where the spondaic alternative is almost unknown. The following lengths must be specifically mentioned:

(tetrameters):

(a) — ⌣⌣   — ⌣⌣   — ⌣⌣   — —

   plurimus in Iunonis honorem   (H. *Od.* i.7.8) cf. **91**)

(b) — ⌣⌣   — ⌣⌣   — ⌣⌣   — ⌣⌣

   te Tyrrhena, pater, rapuit manus.   (Sen. *Oed.* 449)

   [This line, with the last foot invariably a dactyl, is used in series by Seneca, with conspicuous disregard of synaphea (**19**): the final syllable of the line *remains* short instead of being lengthened 'by position' (**13c**) in such cases as

> vivaces hederas remus tenĕt,
> summa ligat vitis carchesia.   (*Oed.* 455–6)]

(tetrameter catalectic):

(c) — ⌣⌣   — ⌣⌣   — ⌣⌣ —

   nenia carmine funero   (Aus. iv.28.7)

('hemiepes', or trimeter catalectic):

(d) — ⌣⌣   — ⌣⌣ —

   arboribusque comae.   (H. *Od.* iv.7.2)

   [Known also as 'lesser archilochean': for its use in 'archilochean' stanzas, cf. **91**. This line is used in series by Ausonius, v. 10.]

(dimeter):

(e) — ⌣⌣   — —

   nubibus atris.   (Boeth. *Cons.* i.7)

   [This line—the equivalent of the last two feet of the hexameter—is used in series by Boethius in the above poem; but much its most important rôle is in aeolic verse, for which cf. **131a**, **139.**]

91. *All-dactylic stanza forms.* Various combinations of the lengths listed above are occasionally found, either with one another or with the hexameter:

  (a) hexameter alternating with **90a**: e.g. H. *Od.* i.7.25–6

      quo nos cumque feret melior fortuna parente,
        ibimus, o socii comitesque.

      — — — ᴗᴗ — ᴗᴗ — —   — ᴗᴗ — —
      — ᴗᴗ — ᴗᴗ — ᴗᴗ — —

      [This combination is sometimes known as *alcmanian*.]

  (b) hexameter alternating with **90d**: e.g. H. *Od.* iv.7.1–2

      diffugere nives, redeunt iam gramina campis
        arboribusque comae.

      — — — ᴗᴗ — ᴗᴗ — —   — ᴗᴗ — —
      — ᴗᴗ — ᴗᴗ —

      [This combination, sometimes known as 'first archilochean' (cp. **94–96**), has been likened to an elegiac couplet cut short midway through the pentameter.]

  (c) **90b** and **90d** in alternation: e.g. Aus. iv. 25.1–2

      te quoque Dryadiam matertĕrăm
        flebilibus modulis.

      — ᴗᴗ — ᴗᴗ — —   — ᴗᴗ
      — ᴗᴗ — ᴗᴗ —

      [For the quantity of the final syllable in l. 1 cp. note to **90b**.]

  (d) **90d** and **90e** joined in a single line: e.g. Boeth. *Cons.* i.2.1

      heu quam praecipiti mersa profundo
      — ᴗ̈ᴗ — ᴗ̈ᴗ — | — ᴗᴗ — —

Dactyls mingled with other metres

92. Following early Greek poets (such as Archilochus), Horace and his successors sometimes alternate dactylic and iambic elements within the same stanza, or even within the same line. The former fusion is seen in the following examples [known as 'pythiambic'] where the hexameter alternates with

  (a) the iambic dimeter (**40A**) ᴗ̄ — ᴗ —   ᴗ̄ — ᴗ —

  (b) the *pure* iambic trimeter (**33A**) ᴗ — ᴗ —   ᴗ — ᴗ —   ᴗ — ᴗ —

e.g.

(a) nox erat et caelo fulgebat luna sereno
       inter minora sidera.

— ∪ ∪   — —   — —   — —   — ∪ ∪   — —

— — ∪ —   ∪ — ∪ —

(H. Epod. 15.1–2)

(b) altera iam teritur bellis civilibus aetas
       suis et ipsa Roma viribus ruit.

— ∪ ∪   — ∪ ∪   — —   — —   — ∪ ∪   — —

∪ — ∪ —   ∪ — ∪ —   ∪ — ∪ —

(H. Epod. 16.1–2)

[Similarly the late poet Boethius alternates iambic trimeters with dactylic *pentameters*, e.g.

(c) quamvis fluente dives auri gurgite
       non expleturas cogat avarus opes

≍ — ∪ —   ≍ — ∪ —   ≍ — ∪ —

— ∪∪   — ∪∪ —   — ∪∪ — ∪∪ —   (Boeth. *Cons.* iii.3.1–2)

and, in another poem, dactylic tetrameters (**90b**) with iambic dimeters, e.g.

(d) sunt etenim pennae volucres mihi
       quae celsa conscendant poli.

— ∪∪   — ∪∪   — ∪∪   — ∪ ∪

≍ — ∪ —   ≍ — ∪ —   (Boeth. *Cons.* iv.1.1–2)

For Boethius' startling mixture of dactylic with *ionic* elements, cf. **126.**]

Archilochean stanzas

93. A development of this mixture is seen when dactylic and iambic (or trochaic) elements are welded *within the same line.* This occurs in certain stanzas of Horace, called 'archilochean' since their prototypes are found in the Greek lyric poet Archilochus.

(For the 'first' archilochean stanza, cf. **91b.**)

94. *'Second' archilochean.* In this stanza, the dactylic hexameter alternates with a compound line ['iambelegus']

≍ — ∪ —   ≍ — ∪ ≍ ‖ — ∪∪ — ∪∪ —

e.g.   tu vina Torquato move consule pressa meo.

(H. *Epod.* 13.6)

in which an iambic dimeter (**40A**) is followed by a dactylic
'hemiepes' (**90**). The two parts of this second line are regarded
as largely independent: this is shown by the fact that the midpoint is sometimes marked by '*syllaba anceps*' (**19**), as in the
following example

> te manet Assaraci tellus, quam frigida parvi
> findunt Scamandri flumină lubricus et Simois.

$$— \cup\cup \quad — \cup\cup \quad — — \quad — — \quad — \cup\cup \quad — —$$
$$— — \cup — \quad — — \cup \underline{\cup} \mid — \cup\cup — \cup\cup — \qquad \text{(H. } Epod. \text{ 13.13–14)}$$

95. '*Third*' **archilochean.** Here the iambic trimeter (**34A**) alternates with a compound line ['elegiambus']

$$— \cup\cup \quad — \cup\cup \quad \underline{\cup} \mid\mid \underline{\cup} — \cup — \quad \underline{\cup} — \cup —$$

e.g.   scribere versiculos amore percussum gravi.

(H. *Epod.* 11.2)

in which the dactylic 'hemiepes' (**90a**) is followed by an iambic
dimeter (**40A**).

[This compound is thus an inversion of the 'iambelegus' in
the last section. Here also the two parts of the line are regarded
as largely independent: the midpoint may be marked by
'*syllaba anceps*' (**19**), or even by hiatus (**15**), as in the following
example

> simul calentis inverecundus deus
> fervidiore mero ⟩ arcana promorat loco.

$$\cup — \cup — \quad \cup — \cup — \quad — — \cup —$$
$$— \cup\cup — \cup\cup — \rangle\mid — — \cup — \quad — — \cup —$$

(H. *Epod.* 11.13–14)]

96. '*Fourth*' **archilochean.** Here two lengths alternate:
  (a) a compound [known as 'greater archilochean']

$$— \underline{\cup\cup} \quad — \underline{\cup\cup} \quad — \underline{\cup\cup} \quad — \cup\cup \mid — \cup — \cup — —$$

e.g.   solvitur acris hiems grata vice | veris et Favoni

(H. *Od.* i.4.1)

in which a dactylic tetrameter (**90b**) is followed by the trochaic
length — ∪ — ∪ — — [ithyphallic, cf. **55A**].

113

(b) a catalectic iambic trimeter, ⏒ — ∪ —   ⏒ — ∪ —   ∪ — —
(cf. **44A**)

e.g.   solvitur acris hiems grata vice veris et Favoni,
        trahuntque siccas machinae carinas. (H. *Od.* i.4.1-2)
        — ∪ ∪   — ∪ ∪   — —   — ∪ ∪ | — ∪ — ∪ — —
        ∪ — ∪ —   — — ∪ —   ∪ — —

CHAPTER 6

Anapaestic Verse

Anapaestic metron

97. In anapaestic verse (as in iambic and trochaic), the metron or unit of movement is of two feet; basically, therefore, the anapaestic metron = ᵕᵕ — ᵕᵕ —. But in place of the anapaest both the spondee — — and the dactyl — ᵕᵕ are admitted, and (in less strict types of verse) the 'proceleusmatic' ᵕᵕᵕᵕ is also found, so that the full scheme of the two-foot metron is

$$\underset{\smile\smile}{\overset{\smile\smile}{-}} \quad \underset{\smile\smile}{\overset{\smile\smile}{-}}$$

However, as in the case of iambic and trochaic verse, two types may be distinguished:

(**A**) a 'strict' type which follows on the whole the practice of the Greek tragedians in avoiding sequences of four (or more) short syllables; this type is seen, for example, in the tragedies of Seneca, and in other silver Latin poets.

(**B**) a 'free' type in which such sequences are not avoided; this is the prevailing type in Roman comedy.

[**98.** It will therefore be apparent to readers of Chapter 5 that the similarity between iambic and trochaic verse is by no means repeated between dactylic and anapaestic. For (a) in dactyls the unit of movement is the single foot, in anapaests the two-foot metron, (b) in dactyls the first element of the foot is invariably a single long syllable, in anapaests no element of the metron is invariable: the admission of the dactyl (and proceleusmatic) to the anapaestic metron has no counterpart in dactylic verse.]

Anapaestic systems—'strict' type (Seneca, etc.)

99. In the Greek drama, anapaests most commonly occur in 'systems' or series consisting chiefly of dimeters—lines of two anapaestic metra, e.g.

Anapaestic Verse

Μενέλαος ἄναξ ἠδ᾽ Ἀγαμέμνων   ∪∪ — ∪∪ —   — ∪∪ — —

(Aesch. Agamemnon 42)

Occasionally a monometer (or line of one metron) occurs; and each system ends in a 'catalectic' dimeter (i.e. a dimeter with its last syllable suppressed), e.g.

ἦραν στρατιῶτιν ἀρωγάν   — — ∪∪ —   ∪∪ — —

(Agam. 47)

The following short system will serve as an example of this structure:

ὅδε τοι μελάθροις τοῖς βασιλείοις   ∪∪ — ∪∪ —   — ∪∪ — —
τρίτος αὖ χείμων   ∪∪ — — —
πνεύσας γονίας ἐτελέσθη.   — — ∪∪ —   ∪∪ — —

(Aesch. Choephori 1065–7)

This type of system is found occasionally in early Roman drama, e.g.

simul et circum merga sonantibus   ∪∪ — — —   — ∪∪ — ∪∪
excita saxis saeva sonando   — ∪∪ — —   — ∪∪ — —
crepitu clangente cachinnat.   ∪∪ — — —   ∪∪ — —

(Accius, fr. 571)

100. Anapaestic systems in Seneca. Systems of the type just described play a large part in the tragedies of Seneca, with one notable change: he, in common with other Roman poets, abandons the use of the catalectic final line. The following is a typical example of Senecan anapaests:

alius raras cervice gravi   ∪∪ — — —   — — ∪∪ —
portare plagas, alius teretes   — — ∪∪ —   ∪∪ — ∪∪ —
properet laqueos.   ∪∪ — ∪∪ —
picta rubenti linea pinna   — ∪∪ — —   — ∪∪ — —
vano cludat terrore feras.   — — — —   — — ∪∪ —

[In anapaests of this type, the dactyl is particularly common as the first foot of the metron (as in *Phaedr.* 46 above), very rare as the second foot; so that the usual metron scheme is ⏓ ⏖ ⏓ —. Sequences of four (or more) short syllables (very common in

116

Roman comedy, cf. **103**) are carefully avoided in later Latin verse, though a startling exception is found in Ausonius, iv.27:

> et amita Veneria properiter obiit:
> cui brevia melea modifica recino:
> cinis ut placidulus ab opere vigeat,
> celeripes adeat loca tacita Erebi.
>
> ⏑⏑⏑⏑ ⏑⏑⏑⏑ ⏑⏑⏑⏑ ⏑⏑—
> —⏑⏑ ⏑⏑⏑⏑ ⏑⏑⏑⏑ ⏑⏑—
> ⏑⏑— ⏑⏑⏑⏑ ⏑⏑⏑⏑ ⏑⏑—
> ⏑⏑⏑⏑ ⏑⏑— ⏑⏑⏑⏑ ⏑⏑—]

[**101.** In this structure there is a close link between lines, emphasised by strict *synaphea* (**19**): i.e. there is rarely hiatus (**15**) or final *anceps* (**19**) between metra or lines. This *synaphea* is in striking contrast to the practice of Plautus in his longer anapaestic lines—cf. **106–107**.

Diaeresis. On the other hand, word-division (diaeresis, **18**) is almost invariable between metra, in anapaests of this type. For this reason, division of lines into dimeters and monometers is not always easy (or important) to determine; but it seems clear that in one chorus (Sen. *Ag.* 310ff.) dimeters and monometers are made to alternate, e.g.

> generis nostri, Iuppiter, auctor,   ⏑⏑— — —   —⏑⏑— —
>   cape dona libens,   ⏑⏑—⏑⏑—
> abavusque tuam non degenerem   ⏑⏑—⏑⏑—   — —⏑⏑—
>   respice prolem.   —⏑⏑— —   ]

102. *Catalexis: the paroemiac.* The name 'paroemiac' is given to the anapaestic dimeter when it is 'catalectic'—i.e. lacking a final syllable. In the anapaestic systems of Greek drama, this line nearly always takes the form ⏖ ⏕ ⏖ — ⏑⏑— —, and this rhythm is reproduced in the line of Accius (*fr.* 571) quoted above (**99**)

> crepitu clangente cachinnat.

[For the less strict forms of paroemiac found in Plautus, cf. **104** b–c.]

As already stated, the Greek custom of closing anapaestic

Anapaestic Verse

systems with this catalectic form was largely abandoned by the Roman poets. But occasionally the paroemiac appears as an independent length, e.g. Aus. iv.7.1–5

nec germana genitum te	– – – –	˘˘ – –
modulamine nenia tristi	˘˘ – ˘˘ –	˘˘ – –
tacitum sine honore relinquat	˘˘ – ˘˘ –	˘˘ – –
super indole cuius adulti	˘˘ – ˘˘ –	˘˘ – –
magnae bona copia laudis.	– – ˘˘ –	˘˘ – –

Anapaestic systems in Plautus

103. Plautus (in common with other Republican dramatists) employs dimeter systems basically of the type described above. As in the case of comic iambic and trochaic verse (cf. **30B**), scansion and identification are often comparatively difficult, owing to the high frequency of elision (**15**), and also owing to unfamiliar differences in quantity produced by the *brevis brevians* law (**14**), whose influence is particularly strong in comic anapaests. [This earlier and less formalised type of verse also admits other licences not found in the stricter type:

(a) sequences of four or more short syllables are not uncommon—cf. l.8 of example at **104a**.

(b) diaeresis (cf. **101**) is not obligatory between metra: cf. ll.3 and 4 of ex. **104a**.

(c) *synaphea* (cf. **101**) is not regular: there may be hiatus (**15**) between lines, e.g. ll.6–7 and 7–8 of ex. **104a**.]

104. *Plautine examples.* The following examples illustrate Plautus' use of anapaests:

(a) unvaried dimeters (corresponding to the Senecan type, cf. **100**)

furtum ego vidi qui faciebat;	– ˘˘ – –	– ˘˘ – –
noram dominum, id cui fiebat	– – ˘˘ –	– – – –
post ad furem egomet devenio	– – – ˘˘	– – ˘˘ –
ferŏque ĕi condicionem hoc pacto:	˘˘ – – ˘˘	– – – –
'ego ĭstuc furtum sciŏ cui factum est;	˘˘ – – –	˘˘ – – –
nunc mihi si vis dare dimidium,	– ˘˘ – –	˘˘ – ˘˘ –

118

indicium domino non faciam.' — ⌣⌣ — ⌣⌣   — — ⌣⌣ —
is mihi nihil etiam respondit. — ⌣⌣⌣⌣⌣   — — — —

(Pl. *Rud.* 954–9)

(b) similar, but with occasional catalectic lines [paroemiacs, 102] as in the Greek type (cf. 100):

novi ego ĭllum ioculo istaec dicit, — ⌣⌣ — ⌣⌣   — — — —
neque ĭlle sibi mereat Persarum ⌣⌣⌣⌣ — ⌣⌣   — — — —
montis, qui esse aurĕĭ perhibentur, — — — —   ⌣⌣⌣⌣ — —
ut ĭstuc faciat quod tu metuis. ⌣⌣ — ⌣⌣ —   — — ⌣⌣ —
tamĕn si faciat, minime irasci ⌣⌣ — ⌣⌣ —   ⌣⌣ — — —
decĕt neque id inmerito eveniet. ⌣⌣⌣⌣ — ⌣⌣   — ⌣⌣ —

(Pl. *Stich.* 23–8)

[In this type of verse, the scheme of the paroemiac (⏓ ⏒ ⏓ ⏒ ⏓ ⏒ —) is much freer than in the Ausonius type quoted above, 102.]

(c) sequences of paroemiacs. The following example shows a heavy spondaic series followed by a burst of short syllables:

—iam tu piscator factu's? — — — —   — — —
—quam pridem non edisti? — — — —   — — —
—possum scire ex te verum? — — — —   — — —
—potes: hodie non cenabis. ⌣⌣⌣⌣ — —   — — —

(Pl. *Stich.* 317–19)

Longer anapaestic lines in Plautus

105. Besides the anapaestic lengths described above, Plautus makes occasional use of longer lines, known (rather misleadingly[1]) as the octonarius and septenarius. They are better regarded as tetrameters—lines of four two-foot metra of the type described in **97**, the last metron of the septenarius being 'catalectic' (lacking a final syllable):
i.e. 'octonarius' = (basically)

⏓ ⏒ ⏓ ⏒   ⏓ ⏒   ⏓ ⏒   ⏓ ⏒ ⏓ ⏒ ⏓ ⏒ ⏓ —
'septenarius' = (basically)

⏓ ⏒ ⏓ ⏒   ⏓ ⏒   ⏓ ⏒   ⏓ ⏒ ⏓ ⏒ ⏓ ⏒ —

[1 Compare the similarly misleading use of the terms in iambic and trochaic verse—cf. 30B.]

Anapaestic Verse

106. *Anapaestic octonarius.* This line consists of four full metra of the type described in **97**: as in Plautus' dimeter systems, sequences of four or more short syllables are not prohibited. e.g.

quid mihi meliust, quid magis in remst, quam a corpore vitam
ut secludam?
ita male vivo atque ita mihi multae in pectore[1] sunt curae
exanimales.
ita res sĕ ⟩ habent: vitae hau parco, perdidĭ spem qua me
oblectabam.
omnia iam circumcursavi atque omnibŭs latebris perreptavi
quaerere conservam, voce oculis auribus ut pervestigarem.

(Pl . Rud. 220-4)

```
_ u u u u _     _ u u _ _     _ _ _ u u _     _ _ _ _

u u u u _ _     u u u u _ _     _ u u _ _     _ u u _ _

u u _ u u _     _ _ _ _     _ u u _ _     _ _ _ _

_ u u _ _     _ _ _ _     _ u u u u _     _ _ _ _

_ u u _ _     _ _ u u _     _ u u _ _     _ _ _ _
```

[There is almost invariably word-division (diaeresis, **18**) after the second metron (e.g. after *remst* in 220 above): the effect of this is that the line seems to fall apart into two equal dimeters of the type seen in **103-104**, and this effect is emphasised by occasional hiatus (**15**) at the mid-point, e.g. Pl. *Pseud.* 183

domĭ nisi malŭm vostra operast hodie? ⟩ improbāe,
vino modŏ cupidae estis.

```
u u u u u u _     u u _ u u _     _ u u _ _     u u u u _ _
```

A pure anapaest or spondee always occurs at the end of the second and fourth metra: thus a double-short element never directly precedes the central diaeresis, or closes the line, and the exact scheme of the octonarius is consequently

ᴗᴗ ᵕᵕ ᴗᴗ ᵕᵕ ᴗᴗ ᵕᵕ ᴗᴗ — ┆ ᴗᴗ ᵕᵕ ᴗᴗ ᵕᵕ ᴗᴗ ᵕᵕ ᴗᴗ —.]

[1 *Word-accent.* Comic anapaestic verse (in contrast to iambic, cf. 38B) does not object to the clash of word-accent produced when a foot consists of a dactylic word—cf. *péctore, pérdidĭ, ómnia, ómnibus, quaérere, aúribus* in this example. But anapaestic verse *does* follow iambic in avoiding a similar clash where a tribrach word is involved—*ĕt ăgĭtĭs, -quĕ gĕnĕrĕ* are inadmissible as anapaestic feet in Plautine verse.]

107. *Anapaestic septenarius.* This line (one element shorter than the octonarius) consists of four anapaestic metra of the type described in **97**, the last metron being 'catalectic' or lacking a syllable. It is clearly descended from the catalectic tetrameter of Greek comedy, e.g. Ar. *Nubes* 998–9

μηδ' ἀντειπεῖν τῷ πατρὶ μηδέν, μηδ' 'Ιαπετόν καλέσαντα
μνησικακῆσαι τὴν ἡλικίαν, ἐξ ἧς ἐνεοττοτροφήθης.

In Greek comedy, this line always ends with the sequence ∪∪——, and sequences of four (or more) short syllables are practically prohibited. As in the case of his other anapaestic lines, Plautus does not observe such restrictions; this may be seen from the following example:

neque eam usquam invenio neque quŏ { eam neque qua
    quaeram consultumst,
neque quem rogitem responsorem quemquam interea convenio,
neque magĭs solae terrae solae sunt quam haec loca ătque hae
    regiones;
neque si vivit, eam viva umquam quin inveniam desistam.

```
∪∪ — — ∪∪   — ∪∪∪∪ —   ∪∪ — — —   — — —
∪∪ — ∪∪ —   — — — —   — — ∪∪ —   — ∪∪ —
∪∪∪∪ — —   — — — —   — — ∪∪ —   ∪∪ — —
∪∪ — — ∪∪   — — — —   — — ∪∪ —   — — —      (Pl. Rud. 225–8)
```

[There is nearly always word-division (diaeresis, **18**) after the second metron e.g. after *responsorem* in 226 above); and this central point of the line is sometimes emphasised by *syllaba anceps* (**19**) or hiatus (**15**) at the diaeresis, e.g. Pl. *Pseud.* 233, *Mil.* 1055

      iam diu ego huic bene et hic mihi volumus, | et
      amicitiast antiqua.

```
— ∪∪ — ∪∪   — ∪∪∪∪ ⸋ | ∪∪ — ∪∪ —   — — —
```

      exprome benignum ex te ingenium, { urbicape,
      occisor regum

```
— — ∪∪ —   — — ∪∪ — {   — ∪∪ — —   — — —
```

As in the case of the octonarius, a pure anapaest or spondee always occurs at the end of the second metron, before the central diaeresis: thus a double-short element never directly

precedes the diaeresis, nor may it close the line—consequently
the exact scheme of the septenarius is

⏕ ⏕ ⏕ ⏕ ⏕ ⏕ ⏕ — ┆ ⏕ ⏕ ⏕ ⏕ ⏕ ⏑⏑ — .]

108. These longer anapaestic lines (the octonarius and septenarius) tend to be found in each other's company—as at Pl.
Rud. 220–8 (quoted above **106, 107**) where five octonarii are
directly followed by four septenarii, or at *Pseud.* 230–3 where
the lengths alternate.

CHAPTER 7

Bacchiac and Cretic Verse

109. The bacchius ⏑ — — and the cretic — ⏑ — seem (to English readers) less natural units of movement than the metres already discussed; but they have a firmly recognised place of their own in Latin verse. It should be noted, however, that their use is almost entirely confined to comedy; and it is relevant to this point that, in the Greek drama, cretics were used more commonly by Aristophanes the comic poet than by the tragedians, while the bacchius is rare in *all* types of Greek verse and seems to owe its popularisation to Roman poets.

BACCHIAC VERSE

110. Among the rare occurrences of 'pure', unvaried bacchii in Greek verse is Prometheus' outcry at Aesch. *Prometheus* 115

τίς ἀχώ, τίς ὀδμὰ προσέπτα μ' ἀφεγγής;

⏑ — —   ⏑ — —   ⏑ — —   ⏑ — —

—a 'tetrameter', or line of four unvaried bacchii. In Roman comedy, bacchiac lines of various lengths are quite common, but the above length—the tetrameter—is the most regularly found, as in

> bonam atque obsequentem deam atque haud gravatam
> patronam exsequontur benignamque multum.
>
> <div align="right">(Pl. <i>Rud.</i> 261–2)</div>

Shorter lines also occur, e.g.

puellae, sed unde . . .   (Rud. 264)

111. *Bacchiac metron—variant forms.* The pure bacchiac metron ⏑ — — can be varied by the following licences:

(a) lengthening of the opening syllable, giving a molossus — — —, especially at the beginning of the line, as in

> nam vox me precantum huc foras excitavit.
>
> <div align="center">— — —   ⏑ — —   ⏑ — —   ⏑ — —   (Pl. <i>Rud.</i> 260)</div>

123

but also elsewhere in the line, e.g.

> iubemus te salvere, mater.—salvete
>
> ∪ — —   — — —   ∪ — —   — — —   (*Rud.* 263)

(b) resolution of one of the long syllables, giving variant forms ∪ ⌣ — and ∪ — ⌣ : e.g.

> manus mihi date, exurgite a genibus ambae.
> misericordior nulla me est feminarum.
>
> ∪ — ⌣   ∪ — —   ∪ — ⌣   ∪ — —
>
> ∪ ⌣ —   ∪ — —   ∪ — —   ∪ — —   (*Rud.* 280–1)

[(c) much more rarely, the lengthened opening syllable may be resolved, ⌣ — — ; or the licences described in (a) and (b) combine, giving forms such as — ⌣ — and — — ⌣. But these variants never obtrude themselves enough to 'swamp' the essential nature of the verse—as may be seen from the following examples:

> sed haec pauperes res sunt inopesque, puellae
>
> ∪ — —   ∪ — —   — ⌣ —   ⌣ — —   (*Rud.* 282)

> dum servi mei perplacet mi consilium,
> dum rursum haud placet nec pater potïs videtur
>
> — — —   ∪ — —   ∪ — —   — ⌣ —
>
> — — —   ∪ — —   ∪ — ⌣   ∪ — —   (Pl. *Merc.* 348–9)]

112. The full scheme of the bacchiac metron is thus

$$
\left\{
\begin{array}{ll}
\cup - - & \text{or} \quad - - - \\
 & [\,\cap - -\,] \\
\cup \cap - & [\,- \cap -\,] \\
\cup - \cap & [\,- - \cap\,]
\end{array}
\right.
$$

113. *Catalexis and other curtailment*

(a) Occasionally the last element of a line is omitted by the process known as catalexis: e.g.

> olent, salsa sunt, tangere ut non velis.
>
> ∪ — —   ∪ — —   ∪ — —   ∪ —   (Pl. *Poen.* 244)

(b) More startlingly, from time to time there is a similar omission in the *penultimate* metron of a line, e.g.

>   mater, nostrum habes.—oportet
> $--- \quad \smallsmile- \quad \smallsmile--$ (Pl. *Rud.* 289)
>   insectatur omnes domi per aedes
> $--- \quad \smallsmile-- \quad \smallsmile- \quad \smallsmile--$ (Pl. *Cas.* 662)

[It is impossible (and perhaps unimportant) to decide whether this curtailment is a special form of bacchiac 'syncopation', or whether the closing sequence $\smallsmile-\smallsmile--$ should be regarded as an iambic segment (cf. **45B, 46B**). For a similar suppression in the penultimate metron of some cretic lines, cf. **118**.]

[**114.** *Diaeresis.* There is often (but not always) word-division (diaeresis, **18**) after the second metron of a bacchiac tetrameter, as in

>   qui sunt qui a patrona | preces meâ expetessunt?
> $--- \quad \smallsmile-- \quad | \quad \smallsmile-- \quad \smallsmile--$
>   (Pl. *Rud.* 259)

Sometimes the syllable preceding such diaeresis may be short like a final *anceps* (**19**); or hiatus (**15**) at this point may be tolerated. For similar licences in Plautus' iambic, trochaic and cretic verse cf. **43-44B, 48B, 119**.]

CRETIC VERSE

115. Cretic verse is quite common in the lyrics of Greek comedy, e.g. at Aristoph. *Equites* 324–5

> ἆρα δῆτ᾽ οὐκ ἀπ᾽ ἀρχῆς ἐδήλους ἀναί-
> δειαν, ἥπερ μόνη προστατεῖ ῥητόρων
>
> $-\smallsmile- \quad -\smallsmile- \quad -\smallsmile- \quad -\smallsmile-$
> $-\smallsmile- \quad -\smallsmile- \quad -\smallsmile- \quad -\smallsmile-$

As in the case of bacchiac verse (**110**), the commonest cretic length is the tetrameter (or line of four metra)—such as the above examples, or (turning to Latin verse)

>   ilico hinc imus, haud longule ex hoc loco
>   (Pl. *Rud.* 266)

But shorter lines are also found, e.g.

>   servitutis ferunt.   (Pl. *Pseud.* 1108)

116. *Cretic metron—variant forms.* The pure cretic metron — ᴗ — admits the following variants:

(a) lengthening of the central syllable, giving a molossus — — — (though not usually at the end of the line), e.g.

verum longe hinc abest unde advectae huc sumus.[1]

— — —   — ᴗ —   — — —   — ᴗ —

(Pl. *Rud.* 267)

(b) resolution of one of the outside syllables, giving — ᴗ ᷈ or (more frequently) ᷈ ᴗ — : e.g.

te quoque etiam dolis atque mendaciis

— ᴗ ᷈   — ᴗ —   — ᴗ —   — ᴗ —   (Pl. *Pseud.* 932)

ut tuo recipias tecto servesque nos
miseriarumque te ambarum uti misereat

— ᴗ —   ᷈ ᴗ —   — — —   — ᴗ —

᷈ ᴗ —   — ᴗ —   — ᴗ —   ᷈ ᴗ —   (Pl. *Rud.* 276–7)

[Very rarely *both* outside syllables seem to be resolved, as in

unde nos hostias agere voluisti ⁊ huc?

— ᴗ —   — ᴗ —   ᷈ ᴗ ᷈   — ᴗ —   (*Rud.* 273)]

[(c) Occasionally a lengthened central syllable is resolved, — ᷈ — ; or the licences described in (a) and (b) are combined, giving forms such as — — ᷈. But such variants are never common enough to obscure the essential quality of the verse: e.g.

nam hercle si cecidero, vestrum erit flagitium.

— ᴗ —   ᷈ ᴗ —   — ᴗ —   — ᷈ —   (Pl. *Pseud.* 1248)

certo vox muliebris auris tetigit meas.

— — —   ᷈ ᴗ ᴗ᷈[2]   — — ᷈   — ᴗ —   (Pl. *Rud.* 233)]

117. The full scheme of the cretic metron is thus:

$$
\left\{
\begin{array}{ll}
\text{— ᴗ —} \quad \text{or} & \text{— — —} \\
 & [\text{— ᷈ —}] \\
\text{— ᴗ ᷈} & [\text{— — ᷈}] \\
\text{᷈ ᴗ —} &
\end{array}
\right.
$$

[1 But when the end of a molossus foot coincides with word-division, word-accent never falls on the lengthened middle element: thus *únde advéct(ae)*, *cérto vóx* are acceptable, *advéctae*, *vóx cérto* unacceptable. For similar restrictions in iambic and trochaic verse cf. **38B**, **49B**.]

[2 cf. **119**.]

118. *Catalexis and other curtailment*

(a) By the process known as catalexis, a line is docked of its final element. This process is rare in cretic verse, but should perhaps be recognised in cases such as

si cades, non cades, quin cadam tecum.

— ᵕ —   — ᵕ —   — ᵕ —   — —   (Pl. *Most.* 329)

(b) A much commoner, and more surprising, curtailment sometimes occurs in the penultimate metron of a line, which thus ends with the sequence — ᵕ — ᵕ — (rarely — — — ᵕ —): e.g.

—cum corona ebrium Pseudolum tuum
—libere hercle hoc quidem. sed vide statum.

— ᵕ —   — ᵕ —   — ᵕ — ᵕ —   (Pl. *Pseud.* 1287–8)

[It is impossible to say with certainty whether this sequence is to be taken as a special form of cretic 'syncopation'; it is equally possible that it is a short *trochaic* segment (cf. **55B**, and compare the similar problem in bacchiac verse, **113**). The question is at any rate not of vital importance to our appreciation of the metre. There is certainly *some* overlap between cretic and trochaic verse: cretics are sometimes found linked to trochaic metra (cf. **30**) of the form ᷁ ᵕ — —, as in

Ampelisca. —hem quis est?—ego, Palaestra.

— ᵕ —   — ᵕ —   ᷁ ᵕ — —   (Pl. *Rud.* 237)

and the ending — ᵕ ᷁ — (sometimes called thymelicus) may be a variant of this: e.g.

quae mihist spes, qua me vivere velint.

— ᵕ —   — — —   — ᵕ ᷁ —   (*Rud.* 209)]

[**119.** *Diaeresis.* There is usually, but not always, word-division (diaeresis, **18**) after the second metron of a cretic tetrameter, as in

nempe equo ligneo ⋮ per vias caerulas

— ᵕ —   — ᵕ —   ⋮   — ᵕ —   — ᵕ —

(Pl. *Rud.* 268)

The syllable immediately preceding this diaeresis is occasionally short, like a final *anceps* (as probably at *Rud.* 233 quoted above, **116**c); or hiatus may be tolerated in this position, as in

sed boni consili } ecquid in te mihist?
— ᴗ — — ᴗ — — ᴗ — — ᴗ — (*Rud.* 950)

For similar licences in bacchiac verse, cf. **114**; and for iambic and trochaic verse, cf. **43–44B, 48B.]**

120. *Prose rhythm.* It should be noticed that the cretic is of special importance in the analysis of Ciceronian prose clausulae: cf. Appendix A.

Bacchiac and cretic verse in comic lyrics

121. On their frequent appearances in the lyrics of Plautus, runs of bacchii and cretics are usually 'pure' enough to be recognised without difficulty. Sometimes the two metres occur in the same scene (e.g. Pl. *Rud.* 259–89). Occasionally there is an admixture of other rhythms—iambic, trochaic or anapaestic (and cf. on **118**); but the basic character of the verse should still be recognisable, even if analysis of single lines is sometimes difficult.

CHAPTER 8

Ionic Verse

Basic ionic metron, and its simple use

122. The form of verse known as ionic is used by both Greek and Roman poets, though it is by no means as common as most other types. This metre, however, seems to have possessed a far greater 'emotional connotation' than most, being especially associated (in both languages) with scenes of orgiastic excitement and 'orientalism'.

For the most part, ionic verse is based on the metron ⌣⌣ — —, known sometimes as the 'minor ionic', in contrast to the 'major ionic' — — ⌣⌣ (for which cf. **125**); and Horace wrote one ode entirely based on this simple metron, without variation: e.g.

> miserarum est neque amori dare ludum neque dulci
> mala vino lavere, aut exanimari metuentis
>   patruae verbera linguae.

> ⌣⌣ — —   ⌣⌣ — —   ⌣⌣ — —   ⌣⌣ — —
> ⌣⌣ — —   ⌣⌣ — —   ⌣⌣ — —   ⌣⌣ — —
> ⌣⌣ — —   ⌣⌣ — —   (H. *Od.* iii. 12.1–3)

123. *Anacreontic.* To some extent the outside syllables of the metron seem to be variable, ⌣⌣ — — being replaced by ⌣⌣ — ⌣ and — ⌣ — —; and these two alternatives are joined in the form known as 'anacreontic' ⌣⌣ — ⌣   — ⌣ — —, which in Greek verse often occurs as a variant of the 'normal' ionic dimeter, e.g.

> γλυκεροῦ δ' οὐκέτι πολλὸς   ⌣⌣ — —   ⌣⌣ — —
> βιότου χρόνος λέλειπται   ⌣⌣ — ⌣   — ⌣ — —
>   (Anacreon, *fr.* 44 D².5–8)

[The anacreontic is in fact often explained as an ionic dimeter with 'anaclasis'—i.e. the 'breaking-up', or inversion, of the two central syllables.]

Anacreontics are surprisingly rare in Latin verse. [They make up the first part of a stanza form in Claudian's *Fescennina* 2, e.g.

> age cuncta nuptiali
> redimita vere tellus   ∪∪ — ∪   — ∪ — —
> celebra toros eriles,

the stanza concluding in choriambics (**132b**),

> omne nemus cum fluviis,   — ∪∪ —   — ∪∪ —
> omne canet profundum.   — ∪∪ —   ∪ — —]

But the anacreontic is chiefly important for its part in the structure of the galliambic (see next section).

The galliambic

124. This line first appears in Hellenistic Greek poetry as a standardised variety of 'ionic tetrameter', and was adopted into Latin by Varro. Its most important occurrence is in the 'Attis' poem of Catullus (63), whose very subject preserves the traditional association of ionics with scenes of excitement.

As conceived by Catullus, this line seems to consist originally of two anacreontics (**123**), the second lacking its final syllable, as in the line (63.14)

(a) aliena quae petentes velut
    exules loca   ∪∪ — ∪   — ∪ — —   ∪∪ — ∪   — ∪ —

There is invariably word-division between the two parts, as indicated above. But more usually the excitement is intensified by free resolution of the long syllables into double-short, particularly late in the line, e.g.

(b) super alta vectus Attis celeri
    rate maria   ∪∪ — ∪   — ∪ — —   ∪∪ — ∪   ∪∪∪ —   (1)
(c) stimulatus ibi furenti rabie
    vagus animi   ∪∪ — ∪   ∪∪∪ — —   ∪∪ — ∪   ∪∪∪ —   (4)
(d) ubi capita Maenades vi iaci-
    unt hederigerae   ∪∪∪∪∪   — ∪ — —   ∪∪ — ∪   ∪∪∪ —   (23)

Occasionally double-short is *contracted* into long, as in

(e) sectam   meam   exsecutae
    duce me mihi comites   — — ∪   — ∪ — —   ∪∪ — ∪   ∪∪∪ —   (15)
(f) rapidae ducem sequuntur
    Gallae properipedem   ∪∪ — ∪   — ∪ — —   — — ∪   ∪∪∪ —   (34)
(g) iam iam dolet quod egi, iam
    iamque paenitet   — — ∪   — ∪ — —   — — ∪   — ∪ —   (73)

If the text is correct, at l.54 (and possibly 18) the 'anacreontic' type is varied by a 'normal' ionic dimeter (**122**), e.g.

(h) et earum omnia adirem furi-
    bunda latibula   ∪∪ − −   ∪∪ − −   ∪∪ − ∪   ∪∪∪ − (54)

[cf. also Varro's
    tonimus chorus tibi nos, tibi nunc semiviri
    ∪∪ − ∪   − ∪ − −   ∪∪ − −   ∪∪ −   (*fr.* 432B)

and the Greek examples of the galliambic quoted by the metrician Hephaestion show this conception:

Γάλλαι μητρὸς ὀρείης φιλόθυρσοι δρομάδες,
αἷς ἔντεα παταγεῖται καὶ χάλκεα κρόταλα.

    − − −   ∪∪ − −   ∪∪ − −   ∪∪ −

    − − ∪∪   ∪∪ − −   − − ∪∪   ∪∪ −

The same conception may indeed be implied by the position of word-accent in some of the resolved lines quoted above: thus

cĕlĕri rătĕ mărĭā, răbĭē văgŭs ănĭmī seem more attractive than

cĕlĕri rătĕ mărĭā, răbĭē văgŭs ănĭmī.]

But in spite of the variations admitted, the line's electrical effect is never lost.

[*Sotadean*

125. Another Hellenistic form, known as sotadean, makes occasional appearances in Latin poetry. One possible analysis of it is as a 'normal' ionic dimeter + anacreontic (cf. **122–3**), but with the line docked of its opening two short syllables: thus

    has cum gemina compede dedicat catenas,
    Saturne, tibi Zoilus, anulos priores

    − −   ∪∪ − −   ∪∪ − ∪   − ∪ − −

                                  (Mart. iii.29)

each line being the equivalent of the Anacreon distich quoted above (**123**), minus the first two syllables.

It is, however, more fashionable to regard the sotadean as exemplifying the use of the 'major ionic' foot − − ∪∪, whose reality as a basis of rhythm—at least in Classical Greek verse—

has been much disputed: an alternative analysis for the above
lines is then

— — ⏑⏑   — —⏑⏑   — ⏑ — ⏑   — —

It need scarcely be stated that the distinction is purely theoretical, and that the important point is the obvious *resemblance* of the sotadean to anacreontics and ionics as met elsewhere.

Sotadeans are occasionally found in the fragments of Ennius and Varro, in Petronius and in Roman comedy, e.g. Pl. *Amph.* 168:

> noctesque diesque assiduo satis superque est

— —   ⏑⏑ — —   ⏑⏑ — ⏑   — ⏑ — —

But in some cases scansion is complicated by sudden resolutions, as in

> ipse dominŭs dives operis, laboris expers   (Pl. *Amph.* 170)
> ita non potui supplicio caput aperire   (Petr. *Satyricon* 132)

— ⏑⏑   ⏑⏑ — —   ⏑⏑ — ⏑   — ⏑ — —

⏑⏑ —   ⏑⏑ — —   ⏑⏑ — ⏑   ⏑⏑⏑ — —]

[*Ionics mingled with other metres*

126. The ionic is on the whole an unsociable metre, and does not mingle readily with other rhythms. The late poet Boethius, however, experimented in some startling mixtures:

(a) an ionic dimeter ⏓⏓ — —   ⏑⏑ — — following a *dactylic* tetrameter catalectic (90c), e.g.

> omne hominum genus in terris simili surgit ab ortu.

— ⏑⏑   — ⏑⏑   —   ⏑⏑   — | ⏑⏑ — —   ⏑⏑ — —

(Boeth. Cons. iii.6.1)

(b) the same length following a *trochaic* dimeter (52A), e.g.

> quod vides sedere celsos solii culmine reges

— ⏑ — ⏓   — ⏑ — — | ⏑⏑ — —   ⏑⏑ — —

(Boeth. Cons. iv.2.1)]

CHAPTER 9

Aeolic Verse

127. *Application of the term 'aeolic'.* Exceedingly common in Greek lyric verse is a range of lines usually termed 'aeolic' because their type is first found in the 'Aeolian' poets Sappho and Alcaeus. Turning to Latin verse, we find this type (though not very frequently) in the *cantica* of Plautus; and much use of it was made by the lyric poets (Catullus, Horace, Statius and Martial), and by Seneca in his tragedies. The nature of 'aeolic' verse is rather easier to grasp in Latin than in Greek lyric, since the Romans largely abandoned the complicated metrical structures of Greek strophes, and tended to confine themselves to a smaller number of standardised lengths.

It would be very wrong to assume that all 'aeolic' lines sprang from the same source, or even that they *need* be analysed in the same fashion. But (whatever their origins) they have certain common features which make it easy for them to occur in the same metrical context; and their grouping and classification, throughout this chapter, are designed solely to show, in the simplest fashion, the common metrical thread running through these lines.

The technical names (e.g. 'asclepiad', 'glyconic') applied to various aeolic lengths are of no help towards an understanding of the metre, and may well be ignored. These names are included in the text, but for reference purposes only.

ELEMENTS OF AEOLIC VERSE

128. *The nucleus.* Unlike the metres described in preceding chapters, aeolic does not run on any regular 'metron-scheme'; but in nearly every aeolic line there is an essential 'nucleus'. This is usually formed by a single choriamb — ⌣ ⌣ —, but

occasionally it is expanded—either into a succession of choriambs — ⏑⏑ — — ⏑⏑ — . . ., or into a dactylic series — ⏑⏑ — ⏑⏑ — ...
The susceptibility of the choriamb to either type of expansion
will be clear from this table:

    — ⏑⏑ —   — ⏑⏑ —   — ⏑⏑ —

    — ⏑⏑ —   — ⏑⏑ —

    — ⏑⏑ —

    — ⏑⏑ — ⏑⏑ —

    — ⏑⏑ — ⏑⏑ — ⏑⏑ —

These types of expansion will be clear from a study of the
nucleus in the following three aeolic lengths (syllables outside
the nucleus can be disregarded for the moment):

(a) H. *Od.* i.8.1
    Lydia, dic per omnis   — ⏑⏑ — | ⏑ — —

(b) H. *Od.* i.8.2
    hoc deos vere, Sybarin cur
        properes amando   — ⏑ — — | — ⏑⏑ —   — ⏑⏑ — | ⏑ — —

(c) H. *Od.* i.9.4
    frigore constiterint acuto   — ⏑⏑   — ⏑⏑ — | ⏑ — —

129. *Syllables preceding and following the nucleus.* The aeolic
nucleus may be preceded and/or followed by a varying number
of syllables. Those that follow the nucleus tend to be alternately
short and long, as in

Cat. 1.1   cui dono lepidum *novum libellum*

    — — | — ⏑⏑ — | ⏑ — ⏑ — —

Elements *preceding* the nucleus are more variable in quantity, at
least in Greek and early Latin lyric; cf. Cat. 1.2–4

    *ari*da modo pumice expolitum?   — ⏑ | — ⏑⏑ — | ⏑ — ⏑ — —
    *Corne*li, tibi: namque tu solebas   — — | — ⏑⏑ — | ⏑ — ⏑ — —
    meas esse aliquid putare nugas   ⏑ — | — ⏑⏑ — | ⏑ — ⏑ — —

But even these elements (as will be seen later) were standardised
by Horace and his successors.

130. *Construction of aeolic lengths.* It will be clear that by combin-
ing the nucleus — ⏑⏑ — (**128**) with different numbers of preceding and following syllables (**129**) a wide variety of lines can be

constructed. Many such lines are rare, especially in Latin lyric; others are particularly common, such as the 'glyconic' $\underline{\smile}\ \underline{\smile}\ |\ -\smile\smile-\ |\ \smile-$, together with its shortened or 'catalectic' form, the 'pherecratean' $\underline{\smile}\ \underline{\smile}\ |\ -\smile\smile-\ |\ -$, as seen in

> huc veni niveo gerens
> luteum pede soccum.   (Cat. 61.9–10)

The variety is wider still when the nucleus $-\smile\smile-$ is expanded into a choriambic or dactylic series (cf. **128**); and, because of this diversity of forms, the aeolic strophes of *Greek* lyric verse are often hard for the beginner to analyse (cf. my *Greek Metre*, **143–144**, for typical examples).

In Latin verse, the range of aeolic lengths actually found is much smaller and consequently little difficulty should be found in analysing them. In the following sections, such lengths as occur are tabulated in such a way as to emphasise the essential nucleus, from which the scansion of aeolic should always start.

With simple nucleus

131.

(a)		— ◡◡ —	—	terruit urbem (H. *Od.* i.2.4) ['Adonic']
(b)		— ◡◡ —	◡ —	te duce concidit (Sen. *Ag.* 866)
(c)		— ◡◡ —	◡ — —	... *edite regibus* (cf. **132c**) (H. *Od.* i.1.1)
				Lydia, dic per omnis (H. *Od.* i.8.1) ['Aristophanic']
				... *cur properes amando* (cf. **132f.**) (H. *Od.* i.8.2)
[(d)		— ◡◡ —	◡ — ◡ —	antevenire nec potis (Pl. *Cas.* 217)]
[(e)	⏓	— ◡◡ —	—	iam noscere possis (Pl. *Aul.* 441)] ['Reizianum']
(f)	⏓ ⏝	— ◡◡ —		Thebae, Bacche, tuae (Sen. *Oed.* 487)
				Maecenas atavis ... (cf. **132c**) (H. *Od.* i.1.1)
(g)	⏓ ⏝	— ◡◡ —	—	grato, Pyrrha, sub antro (H. *Od.* i.5.3) ['Pherecratean']
(h)	⏓ ⏝	— ◡◡ —	◡ —	cui flavam religas comam (H. *Od.* i.5.4) ['Glyconic']
[(i)	⏓ ⏝	— ◡◡ —	◡ — —	educas numerum deorum (Sen. *Ag.* 811)] ['Hipponactean']
(j)	⏓ ⏝	— ◡◡ —	◡ — ◡ — —	cui dono lepidum novum libellum (Cat. 1.1) ['Phalaecian hendecasyllable']
[(k)	⏓ — ⏓	— ◡◡ —		fuisse Penelopam (but cf. **142**) (Pl. *Stich.* 1a)]
(l)	— ◡ — ⏓	— ◡◡ —		et nitoribus nitidis (Pl. *Cas.* 217)
				hoc deos vere, Sybarin ... (cf. **132f.**) (H. *Od.* i.8.2)
[(m)	— ◡ — ⏓	— ◡◡ —	—	imparem aequasti tuus ille (Sen. *Ag.* 812)]
[(n)	— ◡ — ⏓	— ◡◡ —	◡ — —	lucidum caeli decus, huc ades (Sen. *Oed.* 405)]
(o)	— ◡ — ⏓	— ◡◡ —	◡ — —	iam satis terris nivis atque dirae (H. *Od.* i.2.1) ['Sapphic']
[(p)	⏓ — ◡ — ⏓	— ◡◡ —		perrumpet omne servitium (Sen. *Ag.* 605)]
[(q)	⏓ — ◡ — ⏓	— ◡◡ —	—	audetque vitae ponere finem (Sen. *Ag.* 609)]
(r)	⏓ — ◡ — ⏓	— ◡◡ —	◡ —	vides ut alta stet nive candidum (H. *Od.* i.9.1) ['Alcaic 11-syllable']
[(s)	⏓ — ◡ — ⏓	— ◡◡ —	◡ — —	procella fortunae movet aut iniqui (Sen. *Ag.* 594)]

Aeolic Verse

With nucleus expanded by dactyls or choriambs

132.

(a)		— ᵛᵛ — ᵛᵛ —	ᵛ — —	frigore constiterint acuto (H. *Od.* i.9.4) ['Alcaic 10-syllable']
[(b)		— ᵛᵛ — — ᵛᵛ — — ᵛᵛ —	ᵛ — —	delicium, blanditiae, ludus, amor, voluptas (Ausonius ix.4)]
(c)	— —	— ᵛᵛ — — ᵛᵛ —	ᵛ —	Maecenas atavis edite regibus (H. *Od.* i.1.1) ['Lesser asclepiad']
(d)	— —	— ᵛᵛ — — ᵛᵛ — — ᵛᵛ —	ᵛ —	nullam, Vare, sacra vite prius severis arborem (H. *Od.* i.18.1) ['Greater asclepiad']
[(e)	— ᵛ	— ᵛᵛ — ᵛᵛ —	ᵛ — —	tardius celeres agitare currus (Sen. *Ag.* 817)]

(cf. also 133[n].)

(f)	— ᵛ — —	— ᵛᵛ — — ᵛᵛ —	ᵛ — —	hoc deos vere, Sybarin cur properes amando (H. *Od.* i.8.2) ['Greater sapphic']

[**133.** *Contraction in the nucleus.* Very occasionally the nucleus — ◡◡ — is *contracted* to — — —. In Catullus 55 (and 58b), lines with contracted nucleus occur repeatedly among more regular lengths, cf. 55.1–2

oramus, si forte non molestum est,   — — | — — — | ◡ — ◡ — —
demonstres ubi sint tuae tenebrae.   — — | — ◡◡ — | ◡ — ◡ — —

Similarly, Seneca writes one passage in glyconics (**131h**) where the nucleus is occasionally contracted, — ◡ | — ◡◡ — | ◡ — (cf. **137**). It is an affectation almost unknown in Greek aeolic verse[1].]

THE MOST COMMON AEOLIC LENGTHS AND STANZAS

134. The following sections give details of the aeolic lengths most commonly found in Latin lyric, whether used separately or combined in stanzas.

[**135.** *Reizianum.* The aeolic form ⚬⚬ | — ◡◡ — | — ('reizianum'), listed above at **131e**, is a common one in Greek lyric verse, occurring repeatedly (for example) in the anonymous 'swallow song' (*fr.* 32D²) ἦλθ' ἦλθε χελιδών, and frequently throughout the Greek drama.

Like certain other aeolic forms common enough in *Greek* verse, the reizianum seems to have been neglected by the Roman lyric poets; but it has the distinction of being the *only* aeolic form used with any frequency in surviving Roman comedy. Here, however, its aeolic links are largely obscured by the diversity and irregularity of its forms in Plautine verse; moreover, much its strongest association is with iambic surroundings. For this reason, a fuller description of this line will be found under iambic verse—cf. **46B**.]

[[1] It is possible to use the same principle in scanning such lines as Sen. *Agam.* 846

      praebuit saevis tinxitque crudos   — ◡ — — | — (◡◡) — | ◡ — —

and a converse principle of resolution will account for *Agam.* 817

      tardius celeres agitare currus.   — ◡ — (◡◡) | — ◡◡ — | ◡ — —

But for alternative means of analysis cf. **144**, **132e**. The aeolic nature of such lines is clear at any rate, and hypothetical distinctions of analysis should not be taken too seriously.]

136. *Phalaecian hendecasyllable.* This name is given to the aeolic form

$$\underline{\smile}\ \underline{\smile}\ \mid\ -\ \smile\smile\ -\ \mid\ \smile\ -\ \smile\ -\ - \qquad (cf.\ \textbf{131j}).$$

This form is not particularly common in Greek lyric, although it occurs sporadically in the choral odes of tragedy, and is found as an ingredient in Attic *scolia* or drinking-songs; but in Latin it achieved an immense popularity. About two-thirds of Catullus' lyric poems are written in this metre, employed continuously and without variation except in the freedom of the opening syllables:

$$\left.\begin{array}{c}-\ -\\[2pt] -\ \smile\\[2pt] \smile\ -\end{array}\right|\ -\ \smile\smile\ -\ \mid\ \smile\ -\ \smile\ -\ -$$

but even here a spondaic opening is most common, as in

> *passer* mortuus est meae puellae,
>
> *passer*, deliciae meae puellae   (Cat. 3.3–4)

and this opening is sometimes unvaried throughout whole poems.

[In two poems (55 and 58b) Catullus occasionally varies the line by contracting the nucleus $-\smile\smile-$ to $---$: cf. above, **133**.]

This metre was not used by Horace; but later lyric poets, notably Statius and Martial, followed Horace's treatment of other aeolic lengths, and standardised the opening syllables of the phalaecian so that they *always* took the spondaic form. These poets also avoided the use of elision in this line. In consequence of these restrictions, at their hands, the phalaecian acquired a new smoothness which could tend to monotony; and such monotony is accentuated by the tendency (especially in Statius) for word-division to occur at certain points in the line. A regular caesura was in fact established (even in Catullus' phalaecians) at the fifth or sixth syllable. Occasionally the caesura 'rule' has to be broken, in order to accommodate a word which otherwise could not be fitted into the scheme of the line, e.g.

> quae pronos *Hyperionis* meatus   (Stat. *Silv.*i.7.25)
>
> aut dulcem *generasse* Gallionem   (id. ib. 32)
>
> et gratum *popularitate* Magnum   (id. ib. 69)

But on the whole it is remarkable how seldom Statius and Martial admit such words, with the consequent irregularity of caesura. Both 'normal' types of caesura can be seen in the following example, which also illustrates the natural, but monotonous, tendency for certain stereotyped 'word-groups' to form before and after the main caesura.

$$- - \mid - \smile\smile \mid - \; \parallel \; \smile - \smile - -$$

Lucani proprium diem frequentet
quisquis collibus Isthmiae Diones
docto pectora concitatus oestro
pendentis bibit ungulae liquorem.

(Stat. *Silv.* i.7.1–4)

137. *Glyconic stanzas.* In Greek lyric poetry, the commonest of all aeolic lengths is the glyconic $\overset{\smile}{-}\; \overline{\smile} \mid - \smile\smile - \mid \smile -$, with its shortened or 'catalectic' form the pherecratean $\overset{\smile}{-}\; \overline{\smile} \mid$ $- \smile\smile - \mid -$. These two lengths are used, for example, in Anacreon's Hymn to Artemis (*fr.* 1 D²)

γουνοῦμαί σ' ἐλαφηβόλε,
ξανθὴ παῖ Διός, ἀγρίων
δέσποιν' Ἄρτεμι θηρῶν.

These lines were much favoured by the Latin lyric poets.
They are used by Catullus in three poems:

(a) Cat. 17.—each line consists of a glyconic followed by a pherecratean, the scheme in this case being

$$- \overset{\smile}{-} \mid - \smile\smile - \mid \smile - \; \parallel \; - \overset{\smile}{-} \mid - \smile\smile - \mid -$$

e.g.   o Colonia, quae cupis ponte ludere longo.   (17.1)
[This combination is sometimes known as 'priapean' and is also used in the *Appendix Vergiliana, Priapea* 3.]

(b) Cat. 34—stanzas in which three glyconics are followed by a pherecratean.

e.g. montium domina ut fores ⎫
    silvarumque virentium   ⎬ $\overset{\smile}{-}\; \overline{\smile} \mid - \smile\smile - \mid \smile -$
    saltuumque reconditor(um) ⎭
    amniumque sonantum $\overset{\smile}{-}\; \overline{\smile} \mid - \smile\smile - \mid -$

(34.9–12)

[The 'hypermetric' elision of the last syllable of l.11 may be compared with a similar phenomenon in the sapphic stanza, cf. **139.**]

(c) Cat. 61—four glyconics followed by pherecratean

e.g.   cinge tempora floribus
     suave olentis amaraci;
     flammeum cape laetus, huc
     huc veni, niveo gerens
       luteum pede soccum.

$$— \underline{\smile} \mid — \smile\smile — \mid \smile —$$
$$— \underline{\smile} \mid — \smile\smile — \mid —$$

(61.6–10)

The variable opening syllables of these lines were standardised by Horace, in whose works the 'base' is always spondaic[1]; a similar standardisation can be seen in the 'base' of other aeolic lines (cf. **138, 139, 141**). Horace's use of glyconics and pherecrateans is, however, confined to his 'asclepiad' stanzas, for which cf. **138.**

[Seneca (in his tragic choruses) writes whole series of glyconics, with invariably spondaic 'base' $— — \mid — \smile\smile — \mid \smile —$, as at *H.F.* 875–94. In one passage (*Oed.* 882–914) he uses the trochaic form of 'base' and occasionally contracts the nucleus, so that the 'scheme' of line is

$$— \smile \mid — \underline{\smile\smile} — \mid \smile —$$

e.g.   890–1 tuta me media vehat
        vita decurrens via.

For other instances of such contraction in the nucleus, cf. **133, 136.**]

138. *Asclepiad stanzas.* The aeolic lengths known as the 'lesser' and 'greater' asclepiads can be regarded as choriambic 'extensions' of the glyconic described in the last section (cf. also **132** c, d). Their relation with the glyconic and pherecratean

[1 There are two possible (but disputed) exceptions in a probably early Ode—H. *Od.* i.15.24, 36.]

will be clear from this table, which also marks with dotted lines the places at which a caesura is obligatory:

(a)	— —	— ⏑ ⏑ —			—	pherecratean
(b)	— —	— ⏑ ⏑ —			⏑ —	glyconic
(c)	— —	— ⏑ ⏑ — ⋮ — ⏑ ⏑ —			⏑ —	lesser asclepiad
(d)	— —	— ⏑ ⏑ — ⋮ — ⏑ ⏑ —	— ⏑ ⏑ —		⏑ —	greater asclepiad

(As implied above, the spondaic 'base' to these lines is invariable[1].)

Horace's asclepiad stanzas are made up entirely of these four lengths, used either singly or in various combinations as described below. (Although these lines are all common in Greek lyric poetry, Horace himself seems to have been the first to combine them in set stanzas.)

(1) 'First' asclepiad—consists of (c) only, e.g.

> Maecenas atavis edite regibus,
> o ⟩ et praesidium et dulce decus meum,
> sunt quos curriculo pulverem Olympicam
> collegisse iuvat, metaque fervidis . . .
>
> (H. *Od.* i.1.1–4)

[As in all other Horatian odes, the total number of lines must form a multiple of four; this makes corruption virtually certain in *Od.* iv.7, as is also indicated by other irregularities, notably the lack of caesura in l.17

> non incendia Car ⋮ thaginis impiae.

For Seneca's use of this line cf. **143**.]

(2) 'Second' asclepiad—consists of (d) only, e.g.

> nullam, Vare, sacra vite prius severis arborem
> circa mite solum Tiburis et moenia Catili.
> siccis omnia nam dura deus proposuit, neque
> mordaces aliter diffugiunt sollicitudines.
>
> (H. *Od.* i.18.1–4)

This line is also used by Catullus (30), with invariably spondaic base, but without regard for the caesura later standarised by Horace: e.g.

> si tu oblitus es, at di meminerunt, meminit Fides,
> quae te ut paeniteat postmodo facti faciet tui.
>
> (Cat. 30.11–12)

[1 There are two possible (but disputed) exceptions in a probably early Ode—H. *Od.* i.15.24, 36.]

(3) 'Third' asclepiad—(b) and (c) alternate, as in
    donec gratus eram tibi
    nec quisquam potior bracchia candidae
    cervici iuvenis dabat,
    Persarum vigui rege beatior.   (H. *Od.* iii. 9.1–4)

(4) 'Fourth' asclepiad—four-line stanzas of the form cccb;
e.g. quis desiderio sit pudor aut modus
    tam cari capitis? praecipe lugubris
    cantus, Melpomene, cui liquidam pater
    vocem cum cithara dedit.   (H. *Od.* i. 24. 1–4)

(5) 'Fifth' asclepiad—four-line stanzas of the form ccab; e.g.
    Dianam tenerae dicite virgines,
    intonsum, pueri, dicite Cynthium
    Latonamque supremo
    dilectam penitus Iovi.   (H. *Od.* i.21.1–4)
[In these asclepiad combinations, hiatus (**15**) between lines is not excluded, but is relatively uncommon. Hypermetric elision between lines is only found once (H. *Od.* iv. 1.35–6); it is, however, not uncommon for the sense to run on from stanza to stanza.

Some commentators list the five asclepiad systems in a different order—nos. 1, 2, 3, 4, and 5 (as arranged above) becoming respectively 1, 5, 2, 3, 4.]

139. *Sapphic stanza.* The component parts of this stanza are as follows:
(a) The length $- \cup - \overset{\smile}{-} \mid - \cup\cup - \mid \cup - -$ (cf. **1310**), thrice repeated
(b) The 'adonean' $- \cup\cup - \mid -$
This stanza is frequently used by the Aeolian poets Sappho and Alcaeus, e.g.

    φαίνεταί μοι κῆνος ἴσος θέοισιν
    ἔμμεν' ὤνηρ, ὅττις ἐνάντιός τοι
    ἰσδάνει καὶ πλάσιον ἆδυ φωνεί-
    σας ὑπακούει.
                      (Sappho, *fr.* 2 D²)

The ode quoted above was actually translated into Latin sapphics by Catullus (51), who wrote one other poem also (11) in this metre—e.g. 11.5–8

> sive in Hyrcanos Arabasve molles,
> seu Sagas sagittiferosque Parthos
> sive quae septemgeminus colorat
> aequora Nilus.

The sapphic stanza is used very frequently by Horace, e.g.

> integer vitae scelerisque purus
> non eget Mauris iaculis neque arcu
> nec venenatis gravida sagittis,
> Fusce, pharetra.   (H. *Od.* i.22.1–4)

As in other cases, Horace imposes certain new restrictions on the sapphic stanza:

(a) the fourth syllable of the longer line is *always* long

(b) in the longer line, there is always a caesura after *either* the fifth syllable, as in

> integer vitae ⫶ scelerisque purus   — ˘ — — | — ⫶ ˘ ˘ — | ˘ — —

or the sixth syllable, as in

> Mercuri, facunde ⫶ nepos Atlantis   — ˘ — — | — ˘ ⫶ ˘ — | ˘ — —
>
>   (i.10.1)

The latter option is rare in Horace's earlier work, but becomes very common in *Odes*, book iv and *Carmen Saeculare*.

The third and fourth lines of the stanza are regarded as closely connected: occasionally, indeed, there is no word-division between them, e.g.

> Thracio bacchante magis sub inter-
> lunia vento.   (H. *Od.* i.25.11–12)

[There are also a few instances of hypermetric elision between lines (e.g. *C.S.* 47–8); hiatus (**15**) between lines is excluded in *Odes* iv and *Carmen Saeculare*, and is not common in earlier odes.

Statius wrote one poem (*Silv.* iv. 7) in this metre; Seneca uses the sapphic stanza for one tragic chorus (*Med.* 579–606), and also writes whole systems where the longer line is used continuously and without variation (*Phaedr.* 274–324)[1], or

[1 For apparent contraction and resolution of this line in Seneca, cf. **133**[n].]

varied only by an *occasional* adonius to close a sentence (e.g. Med. 607–69).

It is worth noting that Statius and Seneca *always* have word-division at the fifth syllable, and abandon the sixth-syllable 'weak' caesura that is rather characteristic of Horace's later work.]

140. '*Greater sapphic*'. In one ode only (i.8) Horace uses a compound bearing some resemblance to the structure of the sapphic line, and sometimes called the 'greater sapphic'. Two aeolic lengths are used in alternation

$$- \cup - - \ \Big| \ - \ \vdots \ \cup \cup - \ \vdots \ - \cup \cup - \ \Big| \ \cup - -$$

[cf. 131c]

[131 k + c = 132f]

e.g.　　　　　　　　Lydia, dic per omnis

　　hoc deos vere, ⋮ Sybarin ⋮ cur properes amando　　　(1–2)

(In the longer line, there is always a caesura at the points indicated by dotted lines.)

[The appellation 'greater sapphic' is due to the fact that the *first* line may be regarded as a 'regular' sapphic line minus the opening four syllables, the *second* as a 'regular' sapphic with an additional choriamb interpolated. But such niceties may be disregarded, so long as the actual aeolic nature of the lines is appreciated.]

141. *Alcaic stanza*. This stanza, in its original Greek form, is recognisably a mixture of aeolic with iambic-trochaic elements, its component lines being as follows:

(a)　$\overset{\vee}{-} - \cup - \overset{\vee}{-} \ | \ - \cup \cup - \ | \ \cup -$　　　　[cf. 131r] *repeated*

(b)　$\overset{\vee}{-} - \cup - \overset{\vee}{-} \ - \cup - \overset{\vee}{-}$　　　[iambic-trochaic—cf. 45A]

(c)　$- \cup \cup - \cup \cup - \ | \ \cup - -$　　　　　[cf. 132a]

e.g. Alcaeus (*fr.* 91 D²)

οὐ χρῆ κάκοισι θῦμον ἐπιτρέπην·
προκόψομεν γὰρ οὐδ᾽ ἒν ἀσάμενοι,
ὦ Βύκχι, φάρμακον δ᾽ ἄριστον
οἶνον ἐνεικαμένοις μεθύσθην.

This stanza form was adopted and much favoured by Horace; as in the case of other aeolic metres, he and his successors greatly standardised the form of lines, with the result that in (a) and (b) the opening syllables regularly, and the variable middle syllables always, took the long form. This restriction gave a much more weighty effect to the stanza, as may be seen by comparing the previous example with H. *Od.* iii.5.1–4

caelo tonantem credidimus Iovem	(×) — ∪ — — ¦ — ∪∪ — ∪ —	(a)
regnare: praesens divus habebitur	(×) — ∪ — — ¦ — ∪∪ — ∪ —	(a)
Augustus adiectis Britannis	(×) — ∪ — — — — ∪ — —	(b)
imperio gravibusque Persis.	— ∪∪ — ∪∪ — ∪ — —	(c)

Horace also takes unusual care (even for him) in the structure of individual lines. In (a), the caesura (marked above) at the fifth syllable is almost invariable, and exceptions tend to produce a special effect, as at *Od.* i.37.14 *mentemque lymphat* ¦ *am Mareotico* (drunkenness). In (b) (which carries the weight of the stanza) word-ending is almost unknown after the fourth syllable (except in the case of 'forward-looking' monosyllables, as in *devota non͡ extinxit arbos*—not favoured after the fifth syllable (and markedly rarer at this point in *Odes* iii–iv than in i–ii)[1]—very common after the sixth. Consequently the line tends to be centred round a weighty polysyllabic word (or word-group) running from the third or fourth syllable of the line to the sixth or seventh, as in

	Augustus *adiectis* Britannis	above
or	visam *pharetratos* Gelonos	(*Od.* iii.4.35)
or	Titanas *immanemque* turbam	(*Od.* iii.4.43)

In (c) word-ending is not found after the sixth syllable unless there is also a break after the fourth, as in

post equitem ¦ sedet ¦ atra Cura   (*Od.* iii.1.40)

(A more detailed account of these restrictions can be found in many manuals for versifiers.)

[1 The incidence of this word-break is 24 per cent in Odes i–ii, only 8 per cent in iii–iv. It usually marks an appreciable sense-pause, and the line is in most cases concluded with a 'forward-looking' monosyllable + trisyllable, as in

missos ad Orcum; *nec peredit* . . .   (*Od.* iii. 4.75)

much more rarely with two disyllables, of which the first tends to be repeated in the next line, e.g.

pones iambis, *sive flamma*
sive mari libet Hadriano.   (*Od.* i.16.3–4)

hardly ever with any other combination.]

[As in the case of the sapphic stanza (cf. **139**), hiatus (**15**) between lines is uncommon, especially in Horace's later work; synaphea (**19**) is twice (only) emphasised by hypermetric elision—e.g. *Odes* iii. 29.35–6. It is especially typical of this metre for the sense to run on from stanza to stanza, as at *Odes* iv.14.1–24.]

AEOLIC IN DRAMATIC LYRIC

(1) *In comedy*

142. Aeolic plays only a small part in the cantica of Plautus. A reason for this may lie in the complexity of aeolic structure (**128–129**): the tendency throughout comedy (even in cantica) is rather towards repetition of short metrical units, and the only aeolic length which is at all common is the reizianum (**46B**, **135**), which in Plautine usage practically sheds its aeolic affinities. Repetition at its simplest can be seen at *Cas.* 629

> eripite isti gladium quae suïst impos animi
> — ◡◡ —   — ◡◡ —   — ◡◡ —   — ◡◡ —

where the 'nucleus' (**128**), constantly repeated, builds a simple (choriambic) line akin to the cretic run ($-\smile--\smile-\ldots$) which has preceded the line. And Terence (*Ad.* 612ff.) varies a run of such choriambs with 'normal' iambic metra (**30B**)

ut neque quid me faciam	— ◡◡ —	— ◡◡ —
nec quid agam certum siet.	— ◡◡ —	— — ◡ —
membra metu debilia sunt,	— ◡◡ —	— ◠◡ —
animus timore obstipuit.[1]	◠ — ◡ —	— ◡◡ —

[Occasionally more complex patterns are found, but the overall rarity of aeolic in comedy often makes analysis uncertain (as at Pl. *Cas.* 217ff.). Because of this rarity and uncertainty, the whole subject is best ignored by all except specialists; the curious-minded may gain some idea of its pitfalls from a glance

[1 This passage is reminiscent of a regular 'iambo-choriambic' type often found in Aristophanes, e.g. *Nubes* 512–17. Cf. my *Greek Metre*, **50**.]

at Pl. *Stich.* 1ff., which the most natural analysis reduces to short and simple units of a type familiar in Greek lyric:

credo ego miseram	— ᴗ	— ᴗ ᴗ —	(**131f**)
fuisse Penelopam,	ᴗ — ᴗ	— ᴗ ᴗ —	(**131k**)
soror, suo ex animo	ᴗ — ᴗ	— ᴗ ᴗ —	
quae tam diu vidua	— — ᴗ	— ᴗ ᴗ —	
viro suo caruit.	ᴗ — ᴗ	— ᴗ ᴗ —	

But judicious use of *brevis brevians* (**14**) enables from *soror* onwards to be scanned in terms of the Protean reizianum ≍ — ᴗ ᴗ ≍ — (**46B, 135**)—perhaps a preferable alternative in view of Plautus' liking for the length and of the indubitable *versus reiziani* that follow:

. . . soror, suo ĕx animo	ᴗ — ᴗ ᴗ ᴗ —
quae tam diŭ vidua	— — ᴗ ᴗ ᴗ —
viro suŏ caruit.	ᴗ — ᴗ ᴗ ᴗ —
nam nos eĭus animum	— — ᴗ ᴗ ᴗ —
de nostris factis noscimus,	
quarum viri hĭnc apsunt,	

iamb.dim. (**40B**) + — — ᴗ ᴗ — —

quorumque nos negotiis
apsentum, ita ut aequum est

iamb.dim. + — — ᴗ ᴗ — —

sollicitae noctes et dies,
soror, sumu' semper.   *iamb.dim.* + ᴗ — ᴗ ᴗ — —

It should at least be clear from this example that Plautine aeolic must be approached with the greatest caution.]

(2) *In Seneca*

143. The lyrical parts of Seneca's tragedies, with the exception of the anapaestic systems (cf. **100**), are almost entirely written in aeolic verse, which thus achieves a much greater importance than it commands in early comedy (cf. **142**). As already remarked (**6**), such lyrics seldom reach the structural complexity of Greek chorus, nor is there any type of strophic correspondence. Usually whole odes, or sections of odes, are constructed from repetitions of a single line—glyconics (cf. **131h, 137**) as at

Med. 75ff., asclepiads (**132c**) as at *Med.* 56ff., sapphics (**131o**, **139**) as at *Med.* 579ff.

In *Oedipus* and *Agamemnon*, however, there are a few examples of more complex odes, built from a wider variety of metrical units, and resembling the aeolic stanzas of Greek tragedy in nearly all respects except for the lack of antistrophic pattern. Most of these metrical units are centred (after the normal aeolic fashion, cf. **128**) around a central nucleus — ⏑ ⏑ — or its expansions, and their type can be seen in the tables at **131–132**. The metrical scheme of the following example is designed to emphasise the central nucleus, from which analysis should always start:

heu quam dulce malum mor-	— —		— ⏑ ⏑ —	—	(**131g**)
talibus additum			— ⏑ ⏑ —	⏑ —	(**131b**)
vitae dirus, amor, cum pateat malis	— —	— ⏑ ⏑ —	— ⏑ ⏑ —	⏑ —	(**132k**)
effugium et miseros libera mors vocet	— —	— ⏑ ⏑ —	— ⏑ ⏑ —	⏑ —	(**132c**)
portus aeterna placidus quiete.	— ⏑ — —		— ⏑ ⏑ —	⏑ — —	(**131o**)
nullus hunc terror nec impotentis	— ⏑		— — —	⏑ — ⏑ — —[1]	(**131j**)
procella fortunae movet aut iniqui	⏑ — ⏑ — —		— ⏑ ⏑ —	⏑ — —	(**131s**)
flamma Tonantis.			— ⏑ ⏑ —	—	(**131a**)

(*Agam.* 589–95)

[**144.** *Other ingredients in Seneca's aeolic.* In examples **131** l–s, the *comparative* regularity of the syllables preceding the nucleus — ⏑ ⏑ — implies that such lines can be conceived as combinations of iambic or trochaic elements with shorter aeolic units. Thus the 'alcaic 11-syllable' (**131r**) can be analysed

   vides ut alta || stet nive candidum   ⏑ — ⏑ — — (iambic) + — ⏑ ⏑ — ⏑ — (**131b**)

and this analysis is helped, too, by the regularity of word-end at the point indicated (cf. **141**). Following the same principle of word-division, an alternative analysis could be made of the sapphic (**131o**)

   iam satis terris || nivis atque dirae   — ⏑ — — — (trochaic) + ⏑ ⏑ — ⏑ — —

This alternative seems less attractive at first sight, breaking as it does the central nucleus; and such analytical distinctions are at any rate unimportant so far as concerns Horatian lyric. But they *are* of relevance in understanding the more complex aeolic of Seneca, who does seem to have based some of his less familiar aeolic lengths on analyses such as the above: and his lyrics in fact contain lines which are metrical equivalents of

[1 For the contraction of the nucleus — ⏑ ⏑ — to — — — cf. **133, 136**.]

stet nive candidum vides ut alta

and   *nivis atque dirae iam satis terris*

—i.e. inversions of the lines quoted above.

The effect of this theoretical division can be seen in Senecan lines such as the following:

(a) $\smile\!\!- -\smile - -$ latravit ore   (*Agam.* 861: = *vides ut alta.*)

     (repeated) Hebrive ripis pavit tyrannus   (*Agam.* 844)

(b) $- \smile - - - $ decidit caelo   (*Agam.* 851: = *iam satis terris.*)

     (repeated) stipite incusso fregit insultans   (*Agam.* 839)

(c) $\smile\smile - \smile - - $ geminosque fratres   (*Agam.* 837: = *nivis atque dirae*)

     (repeated) vetuitque collo pereunte nasci   (*Agam.* 838)

Similarly they may be linked together or joined with other aeolic lengths:

$\smile\smile - \smile - - \quad - - \smile - - $ gemuitque taurus Dictaea linquens

(*Agam.* 833 = c + a)

$- - \smile - - \quad \smile\smile - \smile - - $ et sensit arcus iterum timendos

(*Agam.* 865 = a + c)

$\smile\smile - \smile - - \quad - \smile - - - $ tibi concitatus substitit mundus

(*Agam.* 827 = c + b)

$- - \smile - - \quad - \smile - - - $ fatale munus duximus nostra

(*Agam.* 628 = a + b)

$- \smile - - - \quad - - \smile - -^1 $ praebuit saevis tinxitque crudos

(*Agam.* 846 = b + a)

$- \smile\smile - \smile - \quad - - \smile - - $ extimuit manus insueta carpi

(*Agam.* 852 = **131**b + **144**a)

Compounds such as the above occur sporadically among the more familiar types described in **143**, and word-division always occurs between the two segments.]

145. The following passage (*Agam.* 626–37) is fairly typical of Seneca's lyrics in their more complex form.

vidimus simulata dona	$- \smile$	$- \smile\smile -$	$\smile - -$ (**131**i)
molis immensae Danaumque	$- \smile - -$	$- \smile\smile -$	$-$ (**131**m)
fatale munus duximus nostra	$\{\begin{matrix} - - \smile - - \\ - - \smile - - \end{matrix}$	$-$	(**144**a + b)
creduli dextra tremuitque saepe	$- \smile - -$	$- \smile\smile -$	$\smile - -$ (**131**o)
limine in primo sonipes, cavernis	$- \smile - -$	$- \smile\smile -$	$\smile - -$ (**131**o)
conditos reges bellumque gestans;	$- \smile - -$	$-$ $- -$	$\smile - -^1$ (**144** b + a)
et licuit dolos versare ut ipsi	$\{\begin{matrix} \\ - - \smile - - \end{matrix}$	$- \smile\smile -$	$\smile -$ (**131**b + **144**a)
fraude sua caderent Pelasgi.		$- \smile\smile - \smile\smile -$	$\smile - -$ (**132**a)
saepe commotae sonuere parmae	$- \smile - -$	$- \smile\smile -$	$\smile - -$ (**131**o)
tacitumque murmur percussit aures,	$\{ - - \smile - -$	$\smile\smile -$	$\smile - -$ (**144** c + a)
ut fremuit male subdolo	$- -$	$- \smile\smile -$	$\smile -$ (**131**h)
parens Pyrrhus Ulixi.	$- -$	$- \smile\smile -$	$-$ (**131**g)

[¹ Cf. also **133**.]

INDEX A

Names of various Metrical Forms and Terms

There are included in this index, for reference purposes, many names which are of no real importance to the understanding of metre, and which have on the whole been avoided in the text of this work. Reference throughout is to sections.

Accent. For the importance of word-accent in Latin verse, cf. especially 10–11, 20–28; for actual principles of accent, 21. For accentual restrictions in individual metres: in saturnian verse—22–25; in iambic and trochaic verse—26, 38B, 49B; in the dactylic hexameter—63, 69, 75; in the elegiac pentameter—88; in anapaests—106[n]; in cretic verse—116[n]. Cf. also **brevis brevians.**

Acephalous (= 'headless'). A term sometimes used to denote the relation of one line to another: thus — ∪ — ∪ — ∪ — can be called an 'acephalous' form of ∪ — ∪ — ∪ — ∪ —. It must be realised that the term has only a relative use, and has no connection with the essential rhythm of a line.

Adonean. The line — ∪ ∪ — —, equivalent to the closing two feet of the dactylic hexameter (60); for its use in dactylic verse, cf. 90e, 91d. (The same length is incidentally *one* variant form of the *anapaestic* metron: cf. 97, 100–101.) For the adonean in aeolic verse (its most common association) cf. 131a, and (on its place in the sapphic stanza) 139.

Aeolic verse. Cf. Ch. 9.

Alcaic. For the alcaic stanza cf. 141, and for its individual lines ('hendecasyllable', 'enneasyllable' and 'decasyllable') and their affinities, cf. 131r, 45A, 132a respectively.

Alcmanian. A name given (a) to the dactylic tetrameter
— ∪∪ — ∪∪ — ∪∪ — — (cf. 90a) (b) to the stanza form in which the
above length alternates with the hexameter (cf. 91a).

Anaclasis. A name sometimes given to the 'breaking up',
or inversion, of syllables: thus the anacreontic (see below) has
been called an 'anaclastic' ionic dimeter. The term is only a
relative one, and bears no relevance to the actual nature of a
metre.

Anacreontic. The line ∪∪ — ∪   — ∪ — —, found in ionic verse as
an 'anaclastic' variant of the dimeter ∪∪ — — ∪∪ — — : cf. 123.
For its part in the structure of the galliambic, cf. 124.

Anacrusis (= 'upbeat'). A term regarded (probably rightly)
with suspicion by scholars. Starting from the assumption that
the main long syllable of a foot carries an ictus or pulse, and re-
presents (in modern musical terms) a 'downbeat', it is possible
to use the term anacrusis to indicate an introductory syllable
'on the upbeat'. (Thus an iambic line can be stated to have an
anacrusis before the first long syllable, ∪ ⋮ — ∪ — ∪ — ∪ —.) At
best the term is only of relative use.

Anapaestic verse (based on the anapaestic metron ∪∪ — ∪∪ —)
cf. Ch. 6. Anapaestic systems—100–104. Longer anapaestic
lines ('octonarius' and 'septenarius') in Plautus—105–108. For
apparent anapaests as variant feet in iambic verse—cf. 34A
and n[1], 35A, 40–42A; 32B, 38B, 40B, 43B, 44B: in trochaic
verse—cf. 47A; 47B, 53B. 'Law of the split anapaest'—
cf. 30B, 38B, 49B. Apparent anapaest opening dactylic hexameter—cf. 61a.

Anceps. An *anceps* or 'doubtful' element is one that may be
short or long—e.g. the first element of the iambic metron
(30A), ⊻ — ∪ —. In 'stichic' lengths, and at the end of a lyric
period, the last element of a line is often of this nature ('final
anceps')—cf. 19. The term *anceps* can also cover vowels in
'doubtful position' before certain combinations of consonants,
where the actual quantity of the syllables is variable—cf. 13d.

Antibacchius. The foot $-\,-\,\smile$, not used in itself as the basis of any rhythm.

Antispast. The sequence $\smile\,-\,-\,\smile$, like the antibacchius not used in itself as a basis for rhythm.

Antistrophe. Cf. 4.

Aphaeresis. Cf. 15.

Apocope. Cf. 13c[n].

Archilochean. This name is given to certain dactylic lines and compounds (first associated with the Greek poet Archilochus), and to their integration in set stanzas, especially by Horace. 'Greater' archilochean line—cf. 55A, 96; 'lesser' archilochean—90d. Archilochean stanza forms—cf. 91b, 93–96. Archilochean dicolon (in Greek verse)—cf. 24, n.[1].

Aristophanean. The length $-\,\smile\smile\,-\;\;\smile\,-\,-$, found occasionally in aeolic: cf. 131c, and (for forms which may be regarded as its extensions) 128, 132 a–b. For its place in the 'greater sapphic' stanza cf. 140.

Arsis and **thesis.** These terms seem originally to have been applied to the upward and downward motion of dancers' feet; subsequently they have been used by ancient and modern metricians to indicate (in modern musical terms) the 'upbeat' and 'downbeat', or the 'stressed' and the 'unstressed' elements of various feet. The whole question of stress or 'ictus' has been much disputed by modern scholars, especially with regard to its presence or absence in *Greek* verse; and there is a further complication in the fact that the terms 'arsis' and 'thesis' have often been misunderstood, and their actual application interchanged. For these reasons the terms have been avoided throughout this work. Cf. footnote to Preface, p. 12.

Asclepiad. The names 'lesser' and 'greater' asclepiad are given to the aeolic lengths $-\,-\;|\;-\,\smile\smile\,-\,-\,\smile\smile\,-\;|\;\smile\,-$ and $-\,-\;|\;-\,\smile\smile\,-\,-\,\smile\smile\,-\,-\,\smile\smile\,-\;|\;\smile\,-$. For the construction of these lengths, cf. 132 c–d; for their use in asclepiad stanzas (sometimes combined with other aeolic forms), cf. 138.

Bacchius. The foot ⌣ — —. As a unit of movement in itself—
cf. 110–114; variant forms of metron, 111–112. Bacchiac verse
in general—109, 121.

Brachycatalexis. See **catalexis.**

Brevis brevians (= 'one short syllable shortening another
syllable'). An important quantitative 'law' in colloquial verse,
notably early comedy. For its formulation and conditions—
cf. 14; for considerations of word-accent—14, 26d. Its frequency
in comic iambics and trochaics—30B; in comic anapaests—103.
(To aid scansion, syllables shortened by this principle are
specially marked as such throughout the text of this book.)

Caesura. Cf. 18. In iambic trimeter and senarius—cf. 36A,
36B; in iambic octonarius and septenarius—43B, 44B. In the
dactylic hexameter—62a, 66–68; in elegiac verse—81a, 83. For
word-division in common aeolic forms—cf. 136, 138–141.

Catalexis. The suppression of the final syllable of a line: thus
the iambic metron ⌣ — ⌣ — has a 'catalectic' form ⌣ — —.
Catalexis in iambics—cf. 44A, B; in trochaics—47A, B, 54A, B.
In dactyls—59, 91; in anapaests—102, 107; in bacchii and
cretics—113, 118; in ionics—124. The term is a relative one
only, and does not help to denote the metrical nature of a line.
(The overworking of this notion can be seen in the invention by
metricians of the terms 'brachycatalexis' to denote a *double* suppression, and 'hypercatalexis' to indicate the opposite process—
i.e. the addition of a syllable to the end of a line.)

Choliambus (= 'limping iambus'). Cf. 42A.

Choriamb. The foot — ⌣ ⌣ —. As the nucleus in aeolic verse—
cf. 128, 130–132. Expanded into a series—128, 132. *Contracted* to
— — —, cf. 133, 136. Mingled with iambic metra in comedy—
142.

Choriambic dimeter. This term can describe the double
choriamb — ⌣ ⌣ — — ⌣ ⌣ — (cf. ex. at 123), but is more often used
of the combinations — ⌣ ⌣ — | ⌣̱ — ⌣̱ — and ⌣̱ ⌣̱ ⌣̱ ⌣̱ | — ⌣ ⌣ —,
in which a choriamb forms one half of the line and the other

syllables are to a large extent variable. Such lines are a great deal commoner in Greek than in Latin verse, but for their occasional appearance in Latin cf. 131d, l.

Clausulae. Cf. Appendix A.

Contraction of double-short into long syllable (as the spondee $--$ can be seen as a contracted form in verses based on the dactyl $-\smile\smile$, Ch. 5 *passim*). For occasional contraction in ionics, cf. 124; in aeolic verse, 133, 136.

Correption. Cf. 15.

Cretic. The foot $-\smile-$. As a unit of movement in itself—cf. 115–119; variant forms of metron—116–117. Cretic verse in general—109, 121. Cretics in Latin prose rhythm—cf. Appendix A. 'Porson's law of the final cretic'—cf. 37A, 48A.

Cyclic dactyls or 'logaoedic dactyls'. A name applied by a now unfavoured school of metrists to dactyls when they appear in aeolic surroundings (cf. exx. at 128, 132a)—where, according to such metrists, their performance is 'hurried' so as to occupy only the same time as trochees. Cf. 12, and see **logaoedic**.

Dactylic verse (based on the dactyl $-\smile\smile$). Cf. Ch. 5. Dactylic hexameter—6ff.; elegiac couplet—78ff.; lyric lengths and combinations—90ff. Dactylic runs in aeolic verse—cf. 128, 132a. For apparent dactyls as variant feet in iambic verse—cf. 34A and n[1], 35A, 40–42A; 33B, 38B, 40B, 43B, 44B: in trochaic verse—cf. 47A; 47B, 53B. In anapaestic verse—cf. 97ff., 106n[2].

Dactylo-epitrite. A form of verse common in the Greek lyric poets, but not (so far as is known) adopted by the Romans. Cf. 7.

Diaeresis, vocalic. Cf. 13c[n].

Diaeresis. Cf. 18. In iambic octonarius and septenarius—cf. 43B, 44B; in trochaic tetrameter, septenarius and octonarius—48A, 48B, 53B; in anapaests—101; in bacchii and cretics—114, 119. Hiatus, etc. at diaeresis—cf. above references, and also 94–95. 'Bucolic diaeresis' in dactylic hexameters—77.

Dimeter (= line of two metra). For dimeters in iambic verse—cf. 40–41A, 40B; in trochaic verse—52A, 52B; in dactylic verse—90e; in anapaestic verse—99ff.; in bacchiac and cretic verse—110, 115; in ionic verse—122.

Dochmius. Basically the length ⌣ — — ⌣ —; with its many variant forms, it plays an important part in Greek dramatic lyric, but seems to have played no part in Latin verse. Cf. 7.

Elegiambus. This name indicates a combination of the dactylic — ⌣⌣ — ⌣⌣ — (as in the elegiac pentameter) with iambics. In Latin verse, it is specifically applied to the length — ⌣⌣ — ⌣⌣ ⌣̲ | ⌣̲ — ⌣ — ⌣̲ — ⌣ —, used by Horace as an ingredient in one of his 'archilochean' stanzas: for this cf. 95. Compare the inverted type of combination known as 'iambelegus', *q.v.*

Elision. Cf. 15. Elision in comic iambic and trochaic verse—cf. 30B, 36B; in Virgil's hexameter—60; in the elegiac couplet—81, 82; in comic anapaests—103. See also **hypermetre.**

Enoplium and **prosodiac.** Two terms variously used to cover a bewildering multitude of lines in Greek lyric verse (see my *Greek Metre*, Index A, *s.v.*); rather mercifully, they are not usually applied to lengths common in Latin verse.

Epitrite. The foot — ⌣ — —, not used as a basis for rhythm in Latin verse (although it is in fact the equivalent of one form of trochaic metron, cf. 30A). For this sequence in Ciceronian clausulae, cf. Appendix A. (The term epitrite is also used of the similar sequences ⌣ — — —, — — ⌣ —, — — — ⌣.)

Epode. Cf. 4.

Foot. Cf. 16, 17, 34A[n].

Galliambic. An ionic length of great variety, for which cf. 124.

Glyconic. The common aeolic length ⌣̲ ⌣̆ | — ⌣⌣ — | ⌣ —: for its place in aeolic verse, cf. 131h. Glyconic stanzas—cf. 137; for its formalisation by Horace, and its place in asclepiad stanzas—138; glyconics in Seneca's tragic lyrics—137, 143.

(In one type of nomenclature, the above length is known as the 'second glyconic', the first and third glyconics being the rarer, but obviously kindred, $- \smile \smile -$ | $\stackrel{\smile}{-} - \stackrel{\smile}{-} -$ and $\stackrel{\smile}{-} \mathrel{\underset{\smile}{\smile}} \stackrel{\smile}{-} \mathrel{\underset{\smile}{\smile}}$ | $- \smile \smile -$, for which see **choriambic dimeter**.)

Hemiepes. A name given to the dactylic $- \smile \smile - \smile \smile -$ (the first part of the epic hexameter and of the pentameter). Cf. 82, 90d.

Hendecasyllable. This term is obviously applicable to any line of eleven syllables, e.g. the first lines of the sapphic and alcaic stanzas (139, 141). But it is particularly associated with the *phalaecian* line, a very common aeolic form, for which cf. 131, and (especially) 136.

Hexameter (= 'six metra'). This term is most commonly used of the *dactylic* hexameter, for which cf. 60ff.

Hiatus. Cf. 15. For hiatus within iambic and trochaic lines of comedy—cf. 43B, 44B, 48B, 53B; as a 'Grecising' affectation in dactylic hexameters—74; within certain dactylic/iambic combinations—95; in anapaestic lines of comedy—106, 107; in bacchiac and cretic verse—114, 119.

Hipponactean. This line is (rather bewilderingly) applied to various lengths supposedly derived from the Greek poet Hipponax:

(a) to the scazon or 'limping line' in iambic and trochaic—cf. 42A, 51A.

(b) to a trochaic/iambic stanza form used by Horace in one ode (ii.18)—cf. 54A.

(c) to the aeolic length $\stackrel{\smile}{-} \mathrel{\underset{\smile}{\smile}}$ | $- \smile \smile -$ | $\smile - -$ (the equivalent of a glyconic with an extra syllable) for which cf. 131 i. This particular length is much less common in Latin than in Greek lyric.

Hypercatalexis. See **catalexis**.

Hypermetre. This term is used to denote the 'overflow' of an elided syllable from one line into the next—a device used occasionally in hexameter verse—cf. 15, 61. For a similar effect in aeolic verse, cf. 19, 136, 138, 139, 141.

Iambelegus. This name implies the mixture of iambic elements with the dactylic — ⌣⌣ — ⌣⌣ — (familiar from the elegiac penta-meter: compare with *elegiambus*, *q.v.*). In Latin verse, it is specifically applied to the length ⌣̱ — ⌣ — ⌣̱ — ⌣ ⌣̱ | — ⌣⌣ — ⌣⌣ —, used by Horace as an ingredient in one of his 'archilochean' stanzas: for this cf. 94.

Iambic verse (based on the iambic metron ⌣ — ⌣ —). Cf. Ch. 4. Two different 'types' of iambic verse—29. '*Type A*' iambic tri-meter—32A–39A; dimeter—40A; trimeter-dimeter combina-tions—41A; 'choliambus' or scazon—42A; catalexis—44A. '*Type B*' iambic senarius—32B–39B; quaternarius—40B; octo-narius—43B; septenarius—44B. Association of iambic with dactylic verse—cf. 92–96. 'Iambic shortening'—*v.s.* **brevis brevians.**

Ictus. See **arsis**, and cf. 12[n].

Ionic verse. Cf. Ch. 8. The 'minor ionic' ⌣⌣ — — and its simple use—cf. 122; anacreontic—123; galliambic—124; sotadean—125. Mixture of ionic with other metres—126.

Ithyphallicus. The length — ⌣ — ⌣ — —, familiar in trochaic verse: cf. 55A, B. For its combination with dactyls ('greater archilochean') cf. 96.

Lecythion. A name given to the 'catalectic' trochaic dimeter — ⌣ — ⌣ — ⌣ — and its variations: cf. 54 A, B. For its use in one stanza-form of Horace, cf. 54A.

Leonine hexameter. Cf. 28n[1].

Logaoedic. A name which was once widely used in describing 'aeolic' verse. Its champions held that all such verse could be scanned to a regular tempo (cf. 12, and see **cyclic dactyls**), and measured most aeolic lines by these rigid and rather pre-sumptuous criteria. (The word logaoedic means literally 'prose-verse'.)

Meiuric (= 'mouse-tailed'). A term applied to a certain class of dactylic lines which end with an inversion . . . — ⌣⌣⌣ — instead of $-\smile\smile-\overset{\smile}{-}$. Such lines are only found, on the whole, in *late* Greek and Latin verse (e.g. Boethius, *Consolatio* iii.1), and have not been included in the scope of this book; they have been regarded as providing an interesting parallel to the scazon, *q.v.*

Metron. Cf. 16, 17: in iambic and trochaic verse, cf. 30 A–B; in dactylic verse, 59; in anapaestic, 97; in bacchiac, 111; in cretic, 116; in ionic, 122.

Molossus. The foot $---$, not a recognised unit of movement in itself. As a variant form in bacchiac and cretic verse—cf. 111, 116; in ionic verse—122, 124; in aeolic verse (contracted from $-\smile\smile-$)—133. For this sequence of syllables in prose clausulae, cf. Appendix A.

Monometer = a line of one metron.

Octonarius (= 'of eight parts'). This term is used to distinguish certain eight-footed lines common in Roman comedy: for the rather illusory distinction of the term from *tetrameter* cf. 31B. Iambic octonarius—43B; trochaic—53B; anapaestic—106.

Paeon. The feet $-\smile\smile\smile$ and $\smile\smile\smile-$ are called *first* and *fourth paeons*. (The second and third paeons exist in theory only.) For their use in bacchiac and cretic verse, cf. 111, 116.

Palimbacchius = *antibacchius, q.v.*

Paroemiac. A name originally applied, perhaps, to the second half of the hexameter, $\overset{\smile}{\underset{\smile}{}}-\smile\smile-\smile\smile--$, but in practice generally used of the (sometimes similar) length which occurs in anapaestic verse as a catalectic dimeter, $\overset{\smile}{-}\overset{\smile}{\smile}\overset{\smile}{-}\overset{\smile}{\smile}\mid\overset{\smile}{-}\overset{\smile}{\smile}-$: for this line in its various forms cf. 99, 102, 104.

Pentameter (= 'five metra'). The second line of the elegiac couplet is generally referred to as the 'dactylic pentameter'—cf. 79–89. (The title is slightly misleading, since—unlike the hexameter—this line does not consist of a fixed number of continuous metra, but of two segments of $2\frac{1}{2}$ metra each $-\overset{\smile}{\smile}-\overset{\smile}{\smile}-\mid-\smile\smile-\smile\smile-$).

Period. Cf. 5.

Phalaecian hendecasyllable (often known simply as *hendeca-syllable*). The aeolic line ⏓ ⏓ | — ⌣⌣ — | ⌣ — ⌣ — —, for whose make-up cf. 131j. For its frequent use by Catullus, Statius and Martial cf. 136.

Pherecratean. The aeolic line ⏓ ⏓ | — ⌣⌣ — | —, for whose make-up cf. 131g. For its common association with glyconics, cf. 137 and see **priapean**; for its place in asclepiad stanzas, cf. 138.

(This line is sometimes called the 'second pherecratean', the term 'first pherecratean' being used of the similar length — ⌣⌣ — | ⌣ — —, for which see **aristophanean**.)

Porson's law. Cf. 37A, 48A.

Priapean. This name is given to the combination of the aeolic lengths known as *glyconic* and *pherecratean*, — ⏓ — ⌣⌣ — ⌣ — | — ⏓ — ⌣⌣ — — : see under these names, and cf. 137a.

Proceleusmatic. The foot ⌣⌣⌣⌣, never used in itself as a basis of movement. For this sequence as a variant foot in iambic verse—cf. 35A, 32B, 43B, 44B; in trochaic verse—47B; in anapaestic verse—97, 100, 103f. Apparent proceleusmatic opening a dactylic hexameter—cf. 61a.

Prodelision. Cf. 15.

Prosodiac. See **enoplium**.

Pyrrhic. The foot ⌣⌣, not used as a basis of rhythm in itself, though the final foot of an iambic line sometimes takes this form due to the licence of final *anceps*, *q.v.*

Pythiambic. This name is given to certain combinations (used particularly by Horace in his *Epodes*) where dactylic and iambic lines alternate; cf. 92.

Quaternarius (= 'of four parts'). This term is used of certain four-footed lines found in Roman comedy; for the rather illusory distinction of the term from *dimeter* cf. 31B. Iambic quaternarius—cf. 40B; trochaic—52B, 54B.

Reizianum. In Greek metre this term is usually confined to the aeolic length ⏓ | — ⏑⏑ — | —, for whose place in aeolic schemes cf. 131e, 135. But in Latin the name is applied more widely to any variant of the scheme ⏓ ⏕ ⏓ ⏕ — ; lines of this type occur quite frequently in comic verse, usually in iambic surroundings. Cf. 46B, 142, and see further under **reizianus**.

Reizianus. The name *versus reizianus* is given to the combination where the above length follows an iambic quaternarius, i.e. (basically)

$$\text{⏒ — ⏑ —} \quad \text{⏒ — ⏑ —} \mid \text{⏓ ⏕ ⏓ ⏕ —}$$

Cf. 46B,142.

Resolution of long syllables into double-short—in iambic and trochaic verse, cf. Ch. 4, *passim*; in bacchiac and cretic verse, cf. 111, 116; in ionics, cf. 124–125.

Rhyme. Cf. 28n[1].

Sapphic. For the 'sapphic hendecasyllable' (the aeolic length — ⏑ — ⏓ | — ⏑⏑ — | ⏑ — —) cf. 131 o, and for its use by Seneca cf. 139 *ad fin.*, 143. Much the commonest association of this line is in the *sapphic stanza*, for which cf. 139. 'Greater sapphic' line and stanza—140.

Saturnian Verse. Cf. 22–25.

Scazon (= 'limping'). For the 'limping' iambic cf. 42A, and for the 'limping' trochaic 51A.

Semi-hiatus = *correption*: cf. 15.

Senarius (= 'of six parts'). This term is especially used of the six-footed iambic line which is the chief dialogue metre of Roman comedy: for this line cf. 32B–39B. For the rather illusory distinction of the term from *trimeter* cf. 31B.

Septenarius (= 'of seven parts'). This term is used of certain lines (found in Roman comedy) which appear to consist of seven feet (more accurately 7½): for the illusory distinction of the term from *tetrameter* (catalectic) cf. 31B. Iambic septenarius —cf. 44B; trochaic—47B–50B; anapaestic—107.

Sotadean. The name of an ionic length occasionally found in lyric verse—cf. 125.

Spondee. The foot $- -$, not a basis of rhythm in its own right. For spandiac feet in iambic verse, cf. 34A and n[1], 35A, 40–42A; 32B, 40B, 43B, 44B: in trochaic verse—cf. 47A; 47B, 53B. For the spondee as a dactylic variant—cf. 58ff.; as an anapaestic variant—97ff.

Stichic verse is verse that runs by the line or στίχος—e.g. the dactylic hexameter—in contrast to longer lyric structures. Cf. 2.

Strophe. Cf. 4.

Suppression. See **syncopation**.

Synaphea. Cf. 19.

Syncopation. This name is given to the apparent suppression of a syllable, such as can often be seen in the iambic verse of *Greek* lyric. As observed in 7, this particular practice does not seem to have been adopted by the Romans. It is possible that a somewhat similar curtailment can be seen in the bacchiac and cretic verse of comedy—cf. 113b, 118b; but the exact principle involved in such curtailment is uncertain.

Synizesis. Cf. 13b, and 13c[n].

System. For systems (or series) in trochaic verse, cf. 52B; anapaestic systems—99ff.

Tetrameter (= line of four metra). This term sometimes over-laps with the terms *octonarius* and *septenarius*, *q.v.*; for the illusory nature of this distinction, cf. 31B. For tetrameters, octonarii and septenarii in iambic verse—cf. 44A; 43B, 44B; in trochaic verse —47A–50A; 47B–50B, 53B; in anapaestic verse—106–108. Dactylic tetrameter—cf. 90; bacchiac—110ff.; cretic—115ff.; ionic—124.

Thesis. See **arsis**.

Thymelicus. A name given to the sequence $- \smile \smile -$ (of indeterminate analysis), sometimes found as an isolated segment, particularly among cretics—cf. 118.

Tribrach. The foot $\smile\smile\smile$: a common resolved variant of the iambus or trochee, cf. Ch. 4, *passim*, especially 34An[1].

Trimeter (= line of three metra). For the iambic trimeter cf. 32A–39A, and for its alternation with other lengths—41A, 92, 95; catalectic trimeter—44A, 54A, 55A, 96. (The iambic senarius—32B–39B—is a closely related by-form of trimeter, and need not be rigidly distinguished from it: cf. 31B.) Dactylic trimeter—cf. 90.

Trochaic verse (based on the trochaic metron $-\smile-\smile$). Cf. Ch. 4. Two different 'types' of trochaic verse—29. '*Type A*' trochaic tetrameter—47A–50A; scazon—51A; dimeter—52A, 54A; ithyphallic—55A. '*Type B*' trochaic septenarius—47B–50B; quaternarius—52B, 54B; octonarius—53B; ithyphallic—55B.

Versus reizianus. See **reizianus.**

Vocalic diaeresis. Cf. 13c[n].

Word-division. For word-division at specific points in various lines, see **caesura** and **diaeresis.** For word-division within resolved elements in iambic and trochaic verse—cf. 38A, 38B, 49A, 49B; in anapaestic verse—106n[2].

INDEX B

References to Authors and Passages

Reference throughout is to sections.
Two dots (..) indicate reference to a continuous passage.

	Sections
ACCIUS	
Fragment	
57¹	99, 102
AESCHYLUS	
Agamemnon	
42	99
47	99
Choephori	
1065..	99
Persae	
155..	47A
Prometheus	
155	110
ALCAEUS	
(cf. also 3, 6, 127)	
Fragment	
91 D²	141
ANACREON	
Fragment	
1 D²	137
44 D², 5..	123
ANTH. LYR. GRAEC.	
(ANON) D²	

	Sections
Fragment	
32 D²	46B, 135
ARCHILOCHUS	
cf. 56A	
ARISTOPHANES	
(cf. also 32B)	
Acharnenses	
840..	46B
Equites	
324..	115
Nubes	
512..	142ⁿ
998..	107
Ranae	
907..	44B
Vespae	
979	32Bⁿ
AUSONIUS	
(cf. also 56A, 64)	
ii.2.1..	40A
iv.7.1..	102
iv.25.1..	91
iv.27	100
iv.28.7	90
ix.4	132

	Sections
BOETHIUS	
(cf. also 56A)	
Consolatio	
i.2.1	91
i.7	90
iii.1 Index A, *s.v.*	
	meiuric
iii.3.1..	92
iii.6.1	126
iv.1.1..	92
iv.2.1	126
CATULLUS	
(cf. also esp. 1, 61,	
62, 64, 68, 69,	
72, 79, 83, 84,	
123, 127, 136–7)	
1.1..	129
3.3	136
4.1..	33A
16	19
18	13
8.1..	42A
11.5..	139
17.1	137
22.19	42A
25.6	44A
29.3..	32A
30.11..	138
34.9..	137
11..	19
51.	139
55.1..	133, 136
58b.	133, 136

	Sections
61.6..	137
9..	130
63.1	124
4	124
14	124
15	124
23	124
34	124
54	124
73	124
64.	68
1	69
78	61
186	13
65.10..	80
66.44..	84
68.112	84
73.6	82
76.8	84
26	83
77.4	83

CICERO
cf. 62, 64, 69, 72,
121, Appendix A

CLAUDIAN
(cf. also 64)

Fescennina

2	123

ENNIUS
(cf. also 1, 62, 64,
65, 70, 79)

Annales

194..	70
230	65
370	70
401..	70
490	61

Varia

14 V	65
42 V	61

	Sections
EURIPIDES	
Medea	
1..	32A

HEPHAESTION
cf. 9[n], 124

HOMER

Odyssey

i.1–2	60

HORACE
(cf. also esp. 1, 19,
40A, 62, 64, 76,
93ff., 127, 138–41)

Epodes

1.29	37A
2.1..	41A
35	34A
61..	41A
9.33	34A
11.2	95
13..	95
13.6	94
13..	94
15.1–2	92
16.	34A
1–2	92
17.	37A[n]
12	34A
53..	34A
78	34A

Odes

i. 1.1..	131, 132, 138
2.1	131, 144
4	131
4.1..	55A, 96
2	44A
9	55A
5.3	131
7.8	90
25..	91
8.1..	128, 131, 140
2	128, 131, 132

	Sections
9.1	131, 144
4	128, 132
10.1	139
15.24	138[n]
36	138[n]
16.3..	141
18.1..	132, 138
21.1..	138
22.1..	139
24.1..	138
25.11..	139
37.14	141
ii. 18.1..	44A, 54A
39	54A
iii. 1.40	141
3.7	45A
4.35	141
43	141
75	141
5.1..	141
9.1..	138
12.1..	122
29.35..	15, 141
iv. 1.35..	138
7.1..	91
2	90
14.1..	141

Satires

i.1.62	76
107..	76
2.38	68
3.4	67

JUVENAL
(cf. also 64, 76)

1.46	76
112	76
159	76

*LIVIUS ANDRONI-
CUS*
(with sundry quota-
tions from *Odyssia*)
—cf. 22–25

LUCAN
cf. 64

LUCRETIUS
(cf. also 61, 64, 71)

	Sections
i.3..	71
13	71
72	67
76	68
87	67
109	67

MARTIAL
(cf. also 35A, 87, 127, 136)

	Sections
i.69.33..	41A
95.	87
iii.22.1..	42A
29.	125

MENANDER
cf. 32B

METELLI
Fragment

1B	24

NAEVIUS
(with quotations from *Bellum Poenicum*)—cf. 22–25.

OVID
(cf. also 61, 64, 77, 81, 86)

Ars Amatoria

i.2	86
14	86
80	28, 86
94	86
ii.24	85

Epistulae ex Ponto

iv.13.44	86

Fasti

	Sections
iii.2	83
11..	89
v.208	78
226	83
582	86

PERVIGILIUM VENERIS

1	47A

PETRONIUS
(cf. also 35A)
Fragment

18 B1..	44A

Satyricon

132	125

PHAEDRUS
cf. 29

PINDAR
cf. 3, 4

PLATO
Fragment

5 D²	79

PLAUTUS
(cf. also esp. 6, 19, 30B, 43B, 48B, 56B, 103ff., 135, 142)

Amphitryo

168	125
170	125

Aulularia

415..	46B
439..	46B
441	131

Bacchides

612	53B

	Sections
968..	52B
974	54B

Casina

217..	131, 142
629	142
662	113
830	55B

Epidicus

3..	54B

Mercator

348..	111

Miles Gloriosus

1055	107

Mostellaria

329	118

Poenulus

244	113
505	48B
818	43B
819	43B

Pseudolus

149..	43B
183	106
191	43B
204..	40B
225..	56B
230..	108
233	107
932	116
1108	115
1248	116
1287..	118

Rudens

47	26, 38B
75	36B
80	36B
89	38B
176	32B
209	118
220..	106

	Sections
225..	107
233	116, 119
237	118
259..	121
259	114
260	111
261..	110
263	111
264	110
266	115
267	116
268	119
273	116
276..	116
280..	111
282	111
289	113
321	44B
324..	44B
329	44B
462	32B
615..	47B
619..	47B
636	48B
650	30B
651	49B
715	47B
738	47B
741	47B
770	49B
775	47B
802	32B
950	119
954..	104
957	14

Stichus

	Sections
1..	131, 142
23..	104
317..	104

PROPERTIUS
(cf. also 83, 85)

	Sections
i.1.2..	85
20.33..	89

SAPPHO
(cf. also 3, 6, 127)

Fragment

	Sections
2 D²	139

SENECA
(cf. also 6, 19, 29, 35A, 47A, 100, 127, 139, 143–5)

Agamemnon

	Sections
310..	101
589..	143
594	131
605	131
609	131
626..	145
628	144
759..	40A
811	131
812	131
817	132, 133
827	144
833	144
837	144
838	144
846	133, 144
851	144
852	144
861	144
865	144
866	131

Hercules Furens

	Sections
255	37A
875..	137

Medea

	Sections
1	35A, 38A
6	35A
14	36A
15..	35A
21	36A
22	37A
37..	35A
43	38A
56..	143
75..	143
99	19

	Sections
579..	139, 143
607..	139
670	35A
746	47A
849	44A
855..	44A

Oedipus

	Sections
229	47A
405	131
449	90
455..	90
487	131
882..	137
890	137

Phaedra

	Sections
43..	100
274..	139
1207..	47A

SILIUS ITALICUS
cf. 64

SOPHOCLES
Ichneutae

	Sections
291	43B

STATIUS
(cf. also 64, 127, 136, 139)
Silvae

	Sections
i.7.1..	136
25	136
32	136
69	136
iv.7	139

TERENCE
(cf. also 30B, 42B, 48B, 142)
Adelphi

	Sections
612..	142

Index B

	Sections
Heauton Timorumenos	
1	32B
9	32B
14	32B
66	36B
100	32B
178	54B
185..	43B
420..	32B, 38B
474	38B
477	32B
481	32B
483	32B
567..	53B
572..	53B
573	49B
Hecyra	
254	44B

TERENTIANUS MAURUS
cf. 9[n]

TIBULLUS
(cf. also 81, 85)

i.3.35..	80

VALERIUS FLACCUS
cf. 61, 64

	Sections
VARRO	
(cf. also 124)	
Fragment	
21B	51A
132B	124
VIRGIL	
(cf. also 61, 64)	
Aeneid	
i.1..	60
1	66, 69
28	66
33	69
87	66
158	66
ii.1	15
9	68
iii.211	13
270	13
658	15, 60
iv.9	67
12	67
41	67
215	74
316	74
385	67
486	68
667	74
v.320	61
481	73

	Sections
vi.602..	61
vii.631	74
viii.452	60
596	60
x.442	73
xi.209	13
614	73
Eclogues	
1.1	27, 72
2	72
5	27
2.42	72
7.53	15, 61
Georgics	
i.153	13
215..	61
322..	77
437	15
ii.344..	15
iii.60	74
344	67
345	66
447	68
iv.50	68
71	73
497	66
Priapea	
3	137

APPENDIX A

A Note on Prose Rhythm and Ciceronian 'Clausulae'

The subject of prose rhythm does not fall strictly within the scope of this book; for—although it is true that certain quantitative sequences seem to have been favoured by ancient prose authors, especially at the ends of sentences—nevertheless such sequences cannot be fitted into the schemes of the individual *metres* described in this book. Recognisable *feet* may of course occur: thus it has been noticed (cf. below) that the cretic foot — ◡ — often occurs near the end of Ciceronian sentences. But such feet are seldom repeated to an extent that would establish an identifiable single metre, and indeed ancient authorities were quick to criticise the suspicion of anything of that nature.

These critics were highly conscious of prose rhythm, in which Plato and the Greek orators had shown some preferences, and which had gathered strength as a subject in the Hellenistic age. But Roman prose writers did not necessarily follow Greek practice. It has been seen elsewhere in this book that the Latin language is rich in quantitatively long syllables; and the consequence of this may be seen in a tendency of the Roman historians to finish sentences with the 'heavy' sequence — — — —. The more fastidious Cicero was more sparing in his use of this and certain other rhythms. Not all Cicero's successors followed his own rhythmical practice, of which some were frankly critical; but later Latin authors such as Quintilian, the younger Pliny and Tacitus in his early *Dialogus* show at least an observable bias towards some of the more favoured Ciceronian endings.

It may at any rate be useful to tabulate certain sequences which *are* common towards the end of Cicero's sentences, or even of his clauses; there is not space to probe deeper into the intricacies of his 'periodic' writing. But both from his remarks (and those of other authors) on the subject, and from the evidence of his actual practice, it is clear that he (and his later imitators) strove after certain 'clausulae', or closing rhythms, and avoided others. Among the latter are dactylic sequences such as the hexameter beginning or ending, $- \smile \smile - - -$ or $- \smile \smile - -$; such closes would be regarded as introducing an undesirable illusion of verse composition. Likewise *long* series of 'pure' iambics or trochaics $- \smile - \smile - \smile -$ ... are very uncommon; but—as will be seen below—*shorter* trochaic sequences are common, and indeed the double-trochee $- \smile - -$ was specially praised by ancient prose critics.

The chief Ciceronian clausulae

The following analysis of clausular elements is to some degree an artificial one, since it splits up what should eventually be regarded as an organic whole. It should *not* be taken as implying that the two parts are separate metrical entities.

(1) *The closing sequence.* It is schematically possible to arrange the most usual Ciceronian closing syllables in a table of *brief* trochaic sequences as follows:

$$
\begin{array}{ll}
\text{(a)} & - \overset{\smile}{-} \\
\text{(b)} & - \smile - \\
\text{(c)} & - \smile - \overset{\smile}{-} \\
[\text{(d)} & - \smile - \smile -]
\end{array}
$$

The first three of these are very common, the fourth less so; longer sequences of this style ($- \smile - \smile - -$, $- \smile - \smile - \smile -$) are—as implied above—unusual.

(2) *The penultimate sequence.* The closing sequences tend also to be preceded by certain syllabic patterns:

$$
\begin{array}{lll}
\text{(A)} & - \smile - & \text{(cretic)}[1] \\
\text{(B)} & - - - & \text{(molossus)} \\
[\text{(C)} & - \smile \smile - & \text{(choriamb)}] \\
[\text{(D)} & - \smile - - & \text{(epitrite)}]
\end{array}
$$

[1 On the extreme frequency of the cretic in this position Zielinski (the pioneer of modern study in this field) based his theory that the cretic is the

Of these only the first—the cretic—commonly precedes the *closing* sequence (a) above; in general, the first two are extremely frequent, the others much less so.

(3) By various combinations of the 'penultimate' and 'closing' sequences, the following common Ciceronian clausulae are obtained.

A+a=	— ˘ —	— —	*e.g.* esse servatam	(Cic. *Verr.* II.v.1)
A+b=	— ˘ —	— ˘ —	(impera) toris opponitur	(id. ib. 2)
A+c=	— ˘ —	— ˘ — —	iudices, providendum	(id. ib. 1)
[A+d=	— ˘ —	— ˘ — ˘ —	(ei)us modi dicere audeas	(id. ib. 5)]
B+b=	— — —	— ˘ —	in partem disputo	(id. ib. 7)
B+c=	— — —	— ˘ — —	cum telo servus esset	(id. ib. 7)
[C+b=	— ˘˘ —	— ˘ —	servitium suspicor	(id. ib. 9)]
[C+c=	— ˘˘ —	— ˘ — —	(vir)tute tua liberatam	(id. ib. 5)]
[D+b=	— ˘ — —	— ˘ —	(in e)quo sedentem viderit	(id. ib. 27)]
[D+c=	— ˘ — —	— ˘ — —	(pe)cunia se liberasse	(id. ib. 23)]

So striking are Cicero's preferences that the five *unbracketed* clausulae above comprise three-fifths of all his oratorical sentence-endings, according to Zielinski's figures.

(4) *Resolutions.* Certain of the long elements in the above sequences resolve readily into double-short: e.g.

A+a (res.) = {	— ˘⏖	— —	esse videatur	(id. ib. 22 *et saepe*)
	⏖ ˘ —	— —	fuerit in bello	(id. ib. 4)
A+b (res.) =	— ˘ —	⏖ —	forte praetereo	(id. ib. 25)
	⏖ ˘ —	— ˘ — , etc.	memoriam foederis	(id.ib. 50)
A+c (res.) = {	⏖ ˘ —	— ˘ — —	fuerit intellegatis	(id. ib. 33)
	— ˘ —	⏖ ˘ — —, etc.	(inter)nuntio redimeretur	(id. ib. 14)
B+b (res.) =	⏖ — —	— ˘ — , etc.	videar rescindere	(id. ib. 20)
B+c (res.) =	— — ⏖	— ˘ — —, etc.	maioribus impetrare	(id. ib. 51)

(Only the first two of these types seem to be particularly common.)

---

basis of most Ciceronian endings. In favour of this, it must be admitted that (B) and (C) (the molossus and choriamb) are occasional substitutes for the cretic in *verse* (cf. **116**). But the analytical value of this theory has often been questioned.]

(5) Cicero also shows certain interesting preferences for word-division within these various clausulae; there is not space to go into these here. But the above notes should serve to indicate the style of sentence-ending that he affected; although (as already stated) it is dangerous to try to break down the different sequences into metrical units.

APPENDIX B

Metrical Notes on Selected Authors

Introductory Note

The aim of this appendix is merely to draw readers' attention to the sections of this book relevant for certain authors and their most widely studied works. It is hoped that with this aid readers will be able to grasp and appreciate the metrical flow of the verse they read.

It has not been thought necessary to give individual references for the commonest metres, such as the dactylic hexameter and elegiac couplet, nor indeed to the iambic and trochaic dialogue metres found in the drama. It would be beyond the scope of this work to explore the metres of very unfamiliar authors; and (with regret) I have confined study of the early Roman poets to the selection in Ernout's *Recueil*, a collection as accessible as any. The authors included in the appendix are accordingly as follows:

(1) Early Roman poets: selections from Ernout's *Recueil*
(2) Plautus
(3) Terence
(4) Catullus
(5) *Appendix Vergiliana*
(6) Horace
(7) Phaedrus
(8) Persius
(9) Seneca
(10) Petronius
(11) Statius
(12) Martial
(13) Ausonius

(1) EARLY ROMAN POETS: SELECTIONS FROM ERNOUT, *Recueil de Textes Latins Archaïques.* (E)

No reference is made to early examples of the dactylic hexameter, for which cf. **6**ff.; nor to the normal dialogue metres of early drama—viz, the iambic senarius (for which cf. **32B**ff.), septenarius (**44B**) and octonarius (**43B**), and the trochaic septenarius (**47B**ff.) and octonarius (**53B**).

For other metres the references below may be helpful:

Saturnians (cf. **22–25**):
> Livius Andronicus 1–27E. (pp. 131–4)
> Naevius 1–33E. (pp. 138–40)

Anapaestic systems (cf. **99**ff.):
> Ennius, *Scenica* 12–18E (p. 174), 57–64E (pp. 177–8), 94–5E (p. 181)
> Pacuvius 62–73E (pp. 202–3)
> Accius 25–6E (p. 208), 95–8E (p. 215)

Cretics (cf. **115**ff.):
> Ennius, *Scenica*, 51–3E (p. 177)

Bacchii (cf. **110**ff.):
> Ennius, *Scenica* 173–6E (p. 191)

(2) PLAUTUS

(a) *Iambic and trochaic dialogue metres.* For these metres (which make up the greater part of Plautus' comedies) the following individual references must suffice:

> Iambic senarius (e.g. *Rud.* 1–184)—cf. **32B**ff.
> Iambic septenarius (e.g. *Rud.* 290–330)—cf. **44B**.
> Iambic octonarius (e.g. *Rud.* 938–44)—cf. **43B**.
> Trochaic septenarius (e.g. *Rud.* 615–63)—cf. **47B**ff.
> Trochaic octonarius (e.g. *Pseud.* 133–7)—cf. **53B**.

These dialogue metres are sometimes interlaced with one another over quite short stretches of writing—e.g. at *Pseud.* 225–9 (troch.oct., troch.sept., iamb.oct., troch.oct., troch.sept.)—and indeed the two octonarii do not often occur unvaried in passages of any length. Consequently recognition, especially of the longer lines, is sometimes difficult; but space does not allow any more detailed references to be given here. (Most editions give a *conspectus metrorum* for individual plays.)

(b) *Cantica*. As stated in Ch. 1 (6) 'strophic' arrangement is uncertain and disputed in Plautus' lyrics; it is certainly hard to see any trace of such arrangement in many cases. The following references may be helpful in indicating the *general* metrical character of individual lyric passages; but it must be realised that exact uniformity of movement is not always to be expected, and lines of the 'dialogue' type are sometimes found among the lyrics. Owing to the rapidity with which one movement can change to another, most of the following references are *only* to passages where the same metre prevails for a reasonable number of lines consecutively (shorter sequences being omitted); and even here the reader must be prepared for the occasional intrusion of lines with a different movement.

Iambic and trochaic (apart from the longer stichic lengths, for which see above):

    Trochaic quaternarius, etc. (cf. **52B**, **54B**)—*Amph.* 575–84, Bacch. 968–74, *Epid.* 3–6.

    Iambic quaternarius (cf. **40B**)—*Pseud.* 204–6; for the combination known as *versus reizianus*, and for the shorter *reizianum* itself (cf. **46B**)—*Aul.* 153–60, 415–45, 752–8, 843–5; *Most.* 858, 891–2; *Rud.* 185, 195–6, 285; *Stich.* 4–8, 772–3; *Truc.* 128–9; and many other isolated instances.

Anapaestic (cf. **104–108**):

    Aul. 149–52, 713–26; *Bacch.* 1076–1108, 1149–1206; *Cas.* 204–12, 217–28, 819–23, 875–82; *Cist.* 203–29, 697–703; *Curc.* 126–32, 138–46; *Men.* 351–68; *Mil.* 1011–93; *Pers.* 168–82, 490–99, 753–96, 843–7; *Poen.* 1174–91; *Pseud.* 165–8, 174–84, 230–42, 592–9, 905–13, 937–50, 1315–29; *Rud.* 220–24, 928–37, 954–62; *Stich.* 16–47, 309–29; *Trin.* 235–42, 256–69, 274–8, 287–92, 820–42, 1115–19; *Truc.* 95–114, 124–7, 603–18.

Bacchiac (cf. **110–114**, **121**) (often with an admixture of iambic elements, cf. **113**):

    Amph. 173–9, 551–73, 633–53; *Aul.* 120–31, 147–8; *Bacch.* 15–19, 618–19, 1120–40; *Capt.* 226–30, 498–509, 781–90, 922–7;

Cas. 144–6 and 152–6, 648–705, 827–42, 855–67; *Cist.* 1–3, 11–13, 20–21, 29–31, 34–7, 673–4, 680–87; *Epid.* 527–30; *Men.* 571–83, 753–72, 966–71; *Merc.* 335–61; *Most.* 85–101, 120–26, 783–803; *Pers.* 805–16; *Poen.* 210–29, 240–57; *Pseud.* 244–58, 1105–6; *Rud.* 189–94, 258–63, 278–82, 906–11, 915–18; *Trin.* 223–32; *Truc.* 211–12, 454–64, 712–21.

Cretic (cf. **115–119, 121**) (often with an admixture of trochaic elements, cf. **118**):

Amph. 219–46; *Asin.* 127–37; *Bacch.* 620–24, 643–68, 1109–15; *Capt.* 205–22, 235–9, 835–6; *Cas.* 147–51, 213–16, 232–5, 641–3; *Curc.* 99–100 and 105–9, 147–54; *Epid.* 85–98, 173–8, 320–3; *Men.* 112–18; *Most.* 108–16, 133–53, 336–44, 690–739; *Pseud.* 920–35, 1116–19, 1285–1314; *Rud.* 207–16, 233–53, 266–77, 664–81; *Trin.* 243–51, 270–3; *Truc.* 582–602, 622–5.

Ionic (sotadeans—cf. **125**): *Amph.* 168–72.

Aeolic (cf. **142**)—(excluding the *reizianum*, for which see above under *iambic*, and cf. **46B**):

Bacch. 626–40, 989–90; *Cas.* 217–18, 937–42, 953–62; *Stich.* 1–9. (But in all these cases analysis is disputed.)

(3) TERENCE

Lyric metres hardly occur in Terence's surviving plays, which are written almost entirely in the regular iambic and trochaic dialogue metres of comedy. (Even anapaests are lacking.) For these the following references must suffice:

Iambic senarius (e.g. *H.T.* 1–174)—cf. **32B**ff.
Iambic septenarius (e.g. *H.T.* 679–707)—cf. **44B**.
Iambic octonarius (e.g. *H.T.* 668–78)—cf. **43B**.
Trochaic septenarius (e.g. *H.T.* 623–67)—cf. **47B**ff.
Trochaic octonarius (e.g. *H.T.* 567–9)—cf. **53B**.

As in the case of Plautus, these dialogue metres are sometimes interlaced with one another over quite short stretches of writing —e.g. at *H.T.* 579ff. (troch.sept., 3 troch.oct., 2 troch.sept., 4 iamb.oct., 2 iamb.sen., then troch.sept.)—and this often makes recognition difficult; but space does not allow any further references to be given here. (Most editions give a *conspectus metrorum* for individual plays.)

Three solitary passages give instances of lyric metres:

Andr. 481–5—chiefly bacchiac (cf. **110ff.**)

Andr. 625–38—chiefly cretic (cf. **115ff.**)

Ad. 610–17—a complex structure: short iambic and trochaic units seem to be mingled with aeolic elements—cf. esp. **142.**

(4) CATULLUS

For Catullus' use of the dactylic hexameter (*poems* 62 and 64) cf. **64**; for his elegiacs (65–116) cf. **82–84**. His lyric metres are covered by the following list of references.

Hendecasyllables (cf. **136**): *poems* 1, 2, 3, 5, 7, 9, 10, 12, 13, 14, 15, 16, 21, 23, 24, 26, 27, 28, 32, 33, 35, 36, 38, 40, 41, 42, 43, 45, 46, 47, 48, 49, 50, 53, 54, 56, 57, 58.

For 55 and 58b, cf. also **133.**

Glyconic combinations (cf. **137**): 17, 34, 61.

Sapphic stanzas (cf. **139**): 11, 51.

Asclepiad ('greater') (cf. **138**): 30.

Iambic trimeter ('pure') (cf. **33A**): 4, 29.

Iambic trimeter ('normal') (cf. **34A**): 52.

Iambic tetrameter (cf. **44Ac**): 25.

Scazon (cf. **42A**): 8, 22, 31, 37, 39, 44, 59, 60.

Galliambic (cf. **124**): 63.

(5) *APPENDIX VERGILIANA* (No reference is made to the dactylic poems.)

Iambic trimeter ('pure') (cf. **33A**): *Priap.* 2, *Catal.* 6, 10, 12.

Iambic trimeter and dimeter alternating (cf. **41A**): *Catal.* 13.

Scazon (cf. **42A**): *Catal.* 2, 5.

Glyconic and pherecratean (cf. **137**): *Priap.* 3.

(6) HORACE (For his Satiric hexameters cf. esp. **64, 67, 76.**)

Sapphic stanza (cf. **139**): *Odes* i. 2, 10, 12, 20, 22, 25, 30, 32, 38;

ii. 2, 4, 6, 8, 10, 16; iii. 8, 11, 14, 18, 20, 22, 27; iv. 2, 6, 11; *Carmen Saeculare.*

Alcaic stanza (cf. **141**): *Odes* i. 9, 16, 17, 26, 27, 29, 31, 34, 35, 37; ii. 1, 3, 5, 7, 9, 11, 13, 14, 15, 17, 19, 20; iii. 1, 2, 3, 4, 5, 6, 17, 21, 23, 26, 29; iv. 4, 9, 14, 15.

Asclepiad stanzas (cf. **138**; as stated there, editors differ in the 'numbering' of the five types of stanza):

(1) *Odes* i.1; iii.30; iv.8.
(2) *Odes* i.11, 18; iv.10.
(3) *Odes* i.3, 13, 19, 36; iii.9, 15, 19, 24, 25, 28; iv.1, 3.
(4) *Odes* i.6, 15, 24, 33; ii.12; iii.10, 16; iv.5, 12.
(5) *Odes* i.5, 14, 21, 23; iii.7, 13; iv.13.

Other stanzas: see under the following references:

Odes. i.4	**96**	*Epodes* 1–10	**41A**
7	**91a**	11	**95**
8	**140**	12	**91a**
28	**91a**	13	**94**
ii.18	**54A**	14, 15	**92a**
iii.12	**122**	16	**92b**
iv.7	**91b**	17	**34A**

(7) PHAEDRUS

The fables are written in free iambic senarii of the comic type, for which cf. **32B**ff.

(8) PERSIUS

His prologue is written in scazons—cf. **42A**. For the satiric hexameter, cf. esp. **64**, **67**, **76**.

(9) SENECA (tragedies, etc.)

Nearly all Seneca's dialogue is written in tragic iambic trimeters, for which cf. **35A**ff.; there are three passages in trochaic tetrameters (*Med.* 740–51, *Phaedr.* 1201–12, *Oed.* 223–32)—cf. **47A**ff.

His lyric passages can be divided under the following headings:

Anapaests (cf. **100ff.**): *H.F.* 125–203, 1054–1137; *Tro.* 67–164, 705–35; *Med.* 301–79, 787–842; *Phaedr.* 1–84, 325–57, 959–88, 1123–7 and 1132–48; *Oed.* 154–201, 432–43, 738–63, 980–97; *Agam.* 57–107, 310–407, 638–58, 664–92; *Thy.* 789–884, 920–69; *H.O.* 173–232, 583–705, 1151–60, 1207–17, 1279–89, 1863–1939, 1944–62, 1983–96; *Oct.* 1–33, 57–99, 201–21, 273–376, 646–89, 762–79, 809–19, 877–983; *Apocolocyntosis* §12.

Dactyls: hexameters at *Med.* 110–15; *Oed.* 233–8, 429–31, 444–8, 466–71.

tetrameters (cf. **90**) at *Phaedr.* 761–3, *Oed.* 449–65.

Iambics: trimeters and dimeters alternating (cf. **41A**) at *Med.* 771–86; dimeters (cf. **40A**) at *Agam.* 759–74; dimeters 'catalectic' (cf. **44A**) after the scheme

$$\text{\Maltese} - \smile - \quad \smile - - \qquad \qquad \textit{Med. } 849\text{–}78^1.$$

Aeolic: for Seneca's use of aeolic in general cf. **143–145**. As stated there, in most cases a single aeolic length is used unvaried in whole series—viz.

Glyconics $- - \mid - \smile\smile - \mid \smile -$ (cf. **137**): *H.F.* 875–94; *Med.* 75–92; *Thy.* 336–403; *H.O.* 1031–1130. For the somewhat different scheme at *Oed.* 882–914 cf. **137** *ad fin.*

Asclepiads $- - \mid - \smile\smile - - \smile\smile - \mid \smile -$ (cf. **138**): *H.F.* 524–91; *Tro.* 371–408; *Med.* 56–74, 93–109; *Phaedr.* 764–823; *Thy.* 122–75; *H.O.* 103–72.

Sapphic stanza (cf. **139**): *Med.* 579–606.

Sapphic 11-syllables $- \smile - - \mid - \smile\smile - \mid \smile - -$ (cf. **139**), in some cases interspersed irregularly with 'adoneans' $- \smile\smile - \mid -$ (as in the regular close to the sapphic stanza above): *H.F.* 830–74; *Tro.* 814–60, 1009–55; *Med.* 607–69 (following regular sapphic stanzas); *Phaedr.* 274–324, 736–60, 1149–53; *Oed.* 110–53, 416–28; *Thy.* 547–622; *H.O.* 1518–1606.

Complex aeolic odes. In only a few instances (*Phaedr.* 1128–31; *Oed.* 405–15, 472–503, 709–37; *Agam.* 589–637, 808–67)

[1 This passage has also been treated as anacreontic—cf. **123**.]

more complex aeolic structures are found, built from a variety of different lengths. For the individual lengths employed, cf. examples in the tables at **131–132**, and **144**; for the structure in general cf. **143–145**, where *Agam.* 589–95 and 626–37 are quoted and analysed.

(10) **PETRONIUS** (Dactylic hexameters and elegiacs are omitted from the following references.)

Occasional verses scattered through the *Satyricon*:

Sat. §   5. Six lines of scazon (cf. **42A**) preceding the hexameters.

§ 15. *ad fin.* Hendecasyllables (cf. **136**).

§ 23. Sotadeans (cf. **125**).

§ 55. (*luxuriae rictu* . . .). Iambic senarii of 'comic' type (cf. **32B**ff.).

§ 79. Hendecasyllables (cf. **136**).

§ 89. 'Tragic type' iambic trimeters (cf. **35A**ff.).

§ 93. Hendecasyllables (cf. **136**).

§ 109 (*infelix* . . .). Hendecasyllables (**136**) following the elegiacs.

§ 132. Sotadeans (cf. **125**).

Fragmenta (*Buecheler*). iv, xx. Hendecasyllables (**136**).

xviii, xxi. Iambic dimeters catalectic (**44A**).

(11) **STATIUS** (Dactylic poems omitted.)

Hendecasyllables (cf. **136**) are found at *Silv.* i.6; ii.7; iv.3, 9.

Alcaic stanza (cf. **141**): *Silv.* iv.5.

Sapphic stanza (cf. **139**): *Silv.* iv.7.

(12) **MARTIAL**

Apart from his dactylic poetry (the greater part of his epigrams are written in elegiacs—cf. esp. **87**), Martial's favourite metre is the *hendecasyllable* (cf. **136**). Poems in hendecasyllables (e.g. i.1,

7, 17, 27, 35, 41) are so numerous that it has been thought unnecessary to list them in full.

Other lyric metres in Martial:

Iambic trimeters (cf. **35A**ff.): vi.12, xi.77.

Iambic trimeters and dimeters alternating (cf. **41A**): i.49, 61; iii.14; ix.77; xi.59.

Scazon (cf. **42A**): i.*praef.*; i.10, 66, 77, 84, 89, 96, 113; ii.11, 17, 57, 65, 74; iii.7, 20, 22, 25, 35, 41, 47, 58, 64, 82, 93; iv.17, 37, 61, 65, 70, 81; v.4, 14, 18, 26, 28, 35, 37, 41, 51, 54; vi.26, 74; vii.7, 20, 26; viii.10, 19, 44, 61; ix.1, 6, 27, 33, 75, 98; x.3, 5, 22, 30, 62, 74, 92, 100; xi.61, 80, 98, 100; xii.10, 13, 32, 34, 51, 57, 65, 81, 87; xiii.61, 81.

Sotadeans (cf. **125**): iii.29.

(13) AUSONIUS

Although Ausonius (4th century A.D.) flourished so long after the poets whose works are listed above, his poems are worth studying as almost the last comprehensive collection of metrical types. (The works of Boethius—150 years later—also repay study in this respect.) The list of references below will show Ausonius' metrical versatility:

Iambic. Senarius ('comic' type trimeter, cf. **32B**ff.): xiii.2–10.

Trimeter ('tragic' type, cf. **35A**ff.): v.15; xviii.25; xix.8, 74; xxii.1 (vii).

Dimeter (cf. **40A**): ii.2, 4, 6; xviii.12, 14 (71–81); xix.48, 98.

Trimeter and dimeter alternating (cf. **41A**): iv.13; v.2, 4, 5, 26; xviii.11, 26, 30 (49ff.), 31 (19ff.); xix.38, 45, 61.

Scazon (cf. **42A**): xviii.15 (19–23); xix.87.

Trochaic. Tetrameter (cf. **47A**ff.): xxii.1 (v).

Tetrameter alternating with iambic trimeter (**35A**): xix.10.

Dactylic (omitting hexameter and elegiac poems):

Hexameter alternating with hemiepes (cf. **91**b): iv.26; ix.2.

Tetrameter alternating with hemiepes (cf. **91c**): iv.25.

Tetrameter catalectic (cf. **90c**): iv.28; xix.89.

Hemiepes (cf. **90d**): v.10.

Dactylic/iambic. Hexameter alternating with iambic dimeter (cf. **92a**): xviii.6, 18.

Anapaests. Dimeters, etc. (cf. **100**): iv.27; v.6, 21.

Paroemiacs (cf. **102**): iv.17.

Aeolic. Hendecasyllables (cf. **136**): vii.1; xviii.7, 14 (82–104), 15 (24–35); xxii.1 (iv).

Sapphics (cf. **139**): ii.1; v.7, 8.

Asclepiads (cf. **138**): xviii.15 (36–56); xxii.1 (iii).

Choriambic expansion (cf. **132b**): ix.4; xxii.1 (vi).

CPSIA information can be obtained
at www.ICGtesting.com
Printed in the USA
LVOW10s0100141117
556186LV00009B/154/P